ROGER EMMERSON was born in Academy. He studied architect the University of Edinburgh an the Glasgow School of Art, gra............ worked in London, Newcastle upon Tyne and, mostly, Edinburgh, running his own practice, ARCHImedia, from 1987 to 1999 while concurrently teaching architectural design at Edinburgh College of Art when he was also visiting lecturer at universities in Venice, Lisbon, Stockholm, Copenhagen and Berkeley. Since 2000 he has worked extensively in the fields of architectural conservation, housing, education and the leisure industries throughout the UK, retiring from architectural practice, although not architecture, in 2016. He is married and lives in Edinburgh close to his four children, their partners and his seven grandchildren. He devotes his free time to writing, painting and playing guitar. On the odd occasion he makes a list, he rarely sticks to it.

By the same author:

Land of Stone: A journey through modern architecture in Scotland, Luath Press, 2022

Scotland in 100 Buildings

ROGER EMMERSON

Luath Press Limited

EDINBURGH

www.luath.co.uk

*My late mother and father drove virtually every road across
a Scotland they loved, visiting many of these buildings and more.
This book's in memory of them.*

First published 2025

ISBN: 978-1-80425-173-7

The author's right to be identified as author of this book
under the Copyright, Designs and Patents Act 1988 has been asserted.

The paper used in this book is recyclable. It is made from
low-chlorine pulps produced in a low-energy, low-emission
manner from renewable forests.

Printed and bound by
Hobbs the Printers Ltd., Totton

Typeset in 9.5 point Sabon by
Main Point Books, Edinburgh

All photographs and illustrations © Roger Emmerson unless otherwise stated.
Text © Roger Emmerson, 2025

Contents

Introduction	9	RENAISSANCE	55
Using the book	11	Craigievar Castle	57
Geographic List of Entries	12	Gladstone's Land	59
Map of Scotland	13	George Heriot's School	61
		Inveraray	63
		Gunsgreen House	65
PREHISTORY	15	Paxton House	67
Skara Brae	17	Stobo Castle	69
Maes Howe	19		
Calanais Standing Stones	21		
Tomnaverie Stone Circle	23	REVIVALISM	71
Ring of Brodgar	25	Royal High School	73
Broch of Gurness	27	Balfour Castle	75
		Cathedral of the Isles	77
		The Blackhouse	79
MEDIAEVAL	29	Gardner's Warehouse	81
St Magnus Cathedral	31	Holmwood	83
Dirleton Castle	33	St Vincent Street UP Church	85
Caerlaverock Castle	35	Lammerburn	87
Lochranza Castle	37	Barclay Bruntsfield Church	89
Crichton Castle	39	Wallace Monument	91
St Machar's Cathedral	41	Kibble Palace	93
Rosslyn Chapel	43	Fountainbridge tenement	95
Kirbuster Farm Museum	45	National Museum of Scotland	97
Claypotts Castle	47	The McManus: Dundee's Art Gallery and Museum	99
Tankerness House	49		
The Study, Culross	51		
Lamb's House	53	Grecian Chambers	101

Mortuary Chapel	103	**EARLY MODERNISM**	151
Queen's Cross Church	105	Scottish National War Memorial	153
St Conan's Kirk	107	Reid Memorial Church	155
John Morgan House	109	St Andrew's House	157
Central Library	111	The Lane House	159
Templeton's Carpet Factory	113	Dunfermline Fire Station	161
Kirkton Cottages	115	Jenners Flats	163
Mansfield Traquair Centre	117	Kirkcaldy Town House	165
		Rothesay Pavilion	167
DÉBUT DE SIÈCLE	119	Palace of Art	169
Melsetter House	121	St Peter-in-Chains RC Church	171
St Vincent Chambers (The Hatrack)	123	Italian Chapel	
Hill House	125	**LATE MODERNISM**	175
Daily Record Printing Works	127	Pitlochry Dam	177
St John the Evangelist RC Church	129	Telephone Exchange	179
		St Paul's RC Church	181
Willow Tea Rooms	131	Canongate Housing	183
Riselaw House	133	Sillitto House	185
Lion Chambers	135	Gala Fairydean Stadium	187
St Peter's RC Church	137	Andrew Melville Hall	189
RW Forsyth's	139	Cumbernauld Town Centre	191
Duke Street Church Halls	141	Edenside Medical Practice	193
John Paris Building	143	Burrell Collection	195
Artist's Studio	145	Eden Court Theatre	197
Grangewells	147	Dundee Repertory Theatre	199
Hippodrome	149	21st-Century Tenement	201
		House for an Art Lover	203

CONTENTS

THE MILLENNIUM   205

    Museum of Scotland   207

    Dundee Contemporary Arts (DCA) 209

    The Scottish Parliament   211

    Homes for the Future   213

    Pier Arts   215

    Sandiefield Housing   217

    Murphy House   219

    The Three Bridges   221

    V&A Dundee   223

    Queen Street Station   225

    Simon Square Housing   227

    Edinburgh Futures Institute   229

Timeline   231

Glossary   241

Bibliography   247

Illustration Credits   255

Acknowledgements   262

Index   263

Introduction

Why *Scotland in 100 Buildings*? Well, there's a unique story here that can be told through the structures that Scots, and others, have erected in Scotland over a period of 5,000 years. Of course, *Scotland in 100 Buildings* is a list. Lists can be fun, sometimes irritating, occasionally infuriating, but also instructive, since what's left out is as significant as what's included. So it would useful for you to know what I mean by 'Scotland' and 'buildings' and how I made my selection.

'Scotland' is the Scotland shown on present-day maps and terminates at the current legal boundary with England. This means I've excluded Berwick upon Tweed although it seems a real Scottish burgh to me.

My definition of a building is any structure erected for human use even if we are not always sure what that use might have been. I've included tombs, funerary monuments and, contentiously perhaps, stone circles, bridges and a sma burgh.

Like many architects, when asked to name a favourite building, I have, often enough, chosen one I have never seen other than as a photograph or drawing in a book; my choice being purely aesthetic or conventional. In giving public talks I would ask that same question of those present. Their choices, almost exclusively have a personal story to tell. Their favourite building is experienced wholly through the context of that story, and not as an object thought of as beautiful or significant in itself. I have adopted the same approach, while hoping also to impart some architectural, aesthetic or historic information.

Buildings do not feature in this list unless I have visited them, preferably have been inside them, although that was not always possible. We all bring our own cultural and personal baggage to our direct sensory experience of a building; my accounts are simply an encouragement, not an instruction.

Architects writing about architecture tend to write for other architects. I've done that myself often enough. Nevertheless, there's no harm in imparting purely architectural information if it's central to explanation, to the story; a little architectural history is a good thing, but more than that is too much.

How should *Scotland in 100 Buildings* be arranged? Should entries be grouped by type – churches, houses, factories – or by location – Glasgow, Eyemouth, Hoy – or by architectural themes – Classicism, Gothicism, Modernism, Expressionism? My aim is to tell a story; so I've adopted a linear narrative with a beginning, middle and provisional end and arranged entries chronologically. Although this is not a history of Scottish architecture, buildings are grouped in eight sections to give some contemporary context: Prehistoric, Mediaeval, Renaissance, Revivalism, Début de Siècle, Early Modernism, Late Modernism and the Millennium.

Using the book

EACH ENTRY GIVES the commonly accepted name for the structure, its location, date and designer, if known. Each building location is numerically identified on the map of Scotland on page 13. Many of the sites have visitor centres and websites describing opening times. Some are private dwellings or simply closed. Please respect the owners' and neighbours' privacy. Some require booking or have severely restricted opening times. Nearby buildings within a roughly 10 minute walk are identified.

While *Scotland in 100 Buildings* is intended as a guide to be dipped into as required, it can equally be read as the story it purports to tell with the section introductions setting the scene.

Geographic List of Entries

Aberdeen 12, 42, 44
Alford 20
Arbroath 41
Ardrossan 73
Bo'ness 60, 62, 63
Caerlaverock 9
Crichton 11
Culross 17
Cumbernauld 82
Dirleton 8
Dundee 15, 39, 86, 90, 97
Dunfermline 68
Edinburgh 18, 20, 21, 26, 33, 34, 37, 38, 45, 48, 53, 55, 57, 58, 59, 61, 64, 65, 66, 67, 69, 76, 78, 79, 89, 91, 95, 99, 100
Eyemouth 23
Fortingall 47
Galashiels 80
Glasgow 30, 31, 32, 36, 40, 46, 50, 52, 54, 56, 72, 84, 87, 88, 92, 94, 98

Glenrothes 77
Helensburgh 51
Inveraray 22
Inverness 85
Kelso 83
Kirkcaldy 70
Lewis 3, 29
Lochawe 43
Lochranza 10
Millport 28
Orkney 1, 2, 5, 6, 7, 14, 16, 27, 49, 74, 93
Paxton 24
Pitlochry 75
Queensferry 96
Roslin 13
Rothesay 71
St Andrews 81
Stirling 35
Stobo 25
Tomnaverie 4

Map of Scotland

Prehistory: 1–6

EMPLOYING A MEASUREMENT from the rule-of-thumb system that includes the 'length of a London omnibus' or the 'size of Wales', 'old as the pyramids' is frequently used to comparatively date other constructions. The pyramids are the obvious signifiers of a complex Egyptian culture which possesses extensive written records – a history – inscribed in hieroglyphs inked, painted or carved on every surface, other than the pyramids, accompanied by copious illustration and statuary. Our knowledge is not complete and mysteries remain.

Scotland's ancient cultures, however, are only imperfectly revealed in stone circles, chambered tombs, brochs, burial goods, pottery and other random objects and in the landscape; nothing is written down. In the strict meaning of the word, then, Scottish cultures are pre-historic even up to quite recent times. Such documentary evidence as exists comes from much later when myth and legend tell of a Celtic hegemony in present-day Scotland, Ireland, Wales and Western France.

Julius Caesar's *Commentarii de Bello Gallico* of 58–49 BCE, about his wars in France, introduced the Druids. In Ireland 8th-century monks collected stories from the oral tradition to assemble a pre-Christian 'history' in the *Lebor Gabála*. One thousand years later, a similar methodology was employed in Scotland by James Macpherson with the publication of four books on the Ossian myth between 1760 and 1765. Each of these texts was designed to satisfy contemporaneous objectives: Caesar's self-aggrandisement; Irish monks' scholasticism; Macpherson's other side of the Enlightenment coin; and for New Age Druids a more earthbound, quasi-democratic belief system. The prevalence of prehistory in Scotland makes for its real presence inscribed in structures in the landscape not text in a book.

Skara Brae

Skara Brae
Bay of Skaill, Orkney, 3180 BCE

SKARA BRAE, PART of the Orkney UNESCO World Heritage Site is, of course, older than the pyramids.

I first visited the location in the early 1980s, in the days before Orkney's tourism boom and status as preferred cruise ship destination, when it was still permissible to wander round within the houses and the connecting passages.

Sat in a house, surrounded by the built-in beds, storage recesses, lamp sconces, shellfish tanks, fire pit and 'dresser', all built from the thin-bed Orkney sandstone due to the scarcity of timber (saved for the roof), the presence of the past in the present was overwhelming. It was entirely possible to reconstruct a life in this setting. I knew where everything should be put, stored or displayed, who sat on which side of the fire pit, slept in which bed, the conversation that might be had, the neighbours one might meet who had just negotiated the sheltering passage to join in.

As a designer, I am captivated by the construction and how the thin-bed 'Walliwall' stone enables considerable manipulation of form in recesses, curves and corbelling and is used either flat 'on bed', or vertically on end to satisfy different constructional needs; house plans vary from nearly square with rounded corners to amorphous, some with cave-like store rooms off the main space. There is no question in my mind that the 'dresser' is anything other than conscious design where decisions were made about thickness of stone, whether laid on bed or vertical, whether presenting on edge or on face and where jointed.

CHECK WEBSITE FOR OPENING TIMES
NEARBY: 14 KIRBUSTER FARM MUSEUM

Maes Howe and the mountains of Hoy beyond

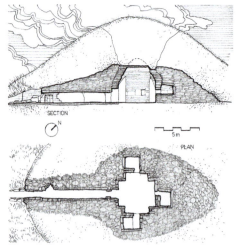

Maes Howe plan and section

Maes Howe

Stenness, Orkney, ca. 2800 BCE

MAES HOWE IS part of the Orkney UNESCO World Heritage Site. It is the largest and most sophisticated of the 'Maes Howe' type of chambered tomb, unique to Orkney. It is aligned with other nearby monuments and there is a Neolithic 'low-road' that connects it to Skara Brae.

The masonry techniques and the implicit design intent evident at Skara Brae have been refined and ordered in plan and section to ratify the sense of a 'holy' space. The constricted entrance passage – roughly 90cm high, less wide, 11m long – is flanked and roofed by single masonry slabs almost the full length of the passage. It opens out into the buttressed square central chamber 4.6m almost the full length of the passage with wall and ceiling masonry now 3.8m high although probably originally 4.6m high, the roof lost first to Viking tomb-robbers and then to James Farrer's crude 19th-century excavation. Three small low-ceilinged crypts open off the centreline of each side but dog-legged so that the interior of each crypt remains hidden. The walls and ceiling/roof of the central chamber, formed of thin-bed Walliwall, are corbelled from just above head-height, beehive fashion, to create a vault. The four supporting buttresses are flanked by single full-height stones which may be repurposed standing stones from a former stone circle on the site, shaped to follow the in-curving line of the ceiling. The tomb has been designed and assembled with some degree of precision. With an obscuring bend in the entryway now missing, Maes Howe is oriented to permit the rays of the sun at the winter solstice to strike the back wall of the chamber. A trilithon, such as is found at Stonehenge, is a feat of engineering; Maes Howe is a work of architecture.

CHECK WEBSITE FOR OPENING TIMES
NEARBY: 5 RING OF BRODGAR

Standing Stones of Calanais

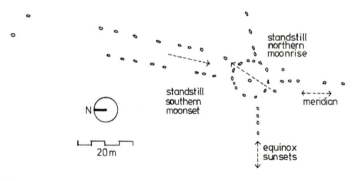

Plan

Calanais Standing Stones
Lewis, ca. 2500 BCE

THE CALANAIS STONES, more properly Calanais 1, are part of several Neolithic structures sited within a matter of a kilometre of each other on the west coast of Lewis. The stones of Lewisian gneiss, 1.7–3.0 billion years old, are erected on an eminence above Loch Roag framed by the hills of Great Bernera to the west and are topographically positioned to focus on the distant landscape form of the sleeping goddess, the Cailleach Na Mointeach. At Calanais the standstill moon rises out of a mountain that looks like a woman lying on her back with her knees raised. The several neighbouring structures, Calanais 2 and 3, suggest this was a centre of significant Neolithic ritual activity.

Calanais 1 is arranged as a small circle with a tall near-central single stone. An 'avenue' of two near parallel lines of stones runs roughly north northeast and shorter single lines of stones run roughly east southeast, south, south southwest and west northwest of the circle. Orientation of the stones suggests that the form is planned astronomically on the rising and setting of the equinoctial sun but principally on the cycle of the moon and on the extreme southern and northern moonrises of the 'standstill' moon that occurs every 18.6 years. The avenue may have been the means by which the celebrants entered the circle.

This is a monument that demands you wander through it, contemplating its complex cosmological and religious purposes and joining in one's progress with the many thousands in earlier times who have made their way to its heart and to the heart of its present mystery.

CHECK WEBSITE FOR OPENING TIMES
NEARBY: 29 THE BLACKHOUSE

Tomnaverie Stone Circle

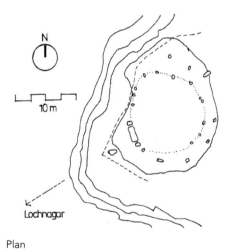

Plan

Tomnaverie Stone Circle
Aberdeenshire, 2500 BCE

TOMNAVERIE IS ONE of the smaller stone circles, ca. 17m across, and sits on a low hill 178m above sea level. It's what is known as a recumbent stone circle from the very large and prominent stone, in this case weighing about 6.5 tons, laid on its side and flanked by two stones taller than the rest. Such recumbent stones tend to be oriented so that one's view, framed by the flanking stones, faces south southwest.

As with all of these monuments there is much speculation about astronomical orientation and the positioning of significant parts of the circle do align with known astronomical events. Ancient peoples were farmers, fishers and hunters for whom knowledge of the seasons was critical. I have to assume they were not unobservant and that their metaphoric book of temporal knowledge and calculation was the sky and the position of the sun, moon, planets and stars within it. Tomnaverie, of course, in addition to the possible astronomic orientation of its several stones, is planned to focus on the gap to the west of Scar Hill which frames Lochnagar (Beinn Chìochan) 30km distant to the south southwest, and which reveals itself as a Cailleach, a sleeping goddess, thereby overlaying further religious and cultural significance on the circle.

CHECK WEBSITE FOR OPENING TIMES

Ring of Brodgar

Ring of Brodgar
Stenness, Orkney, 2500–2000 BCE

THE RING OF Brodgar is part of the Orkney UNESCO World Heritage Site. It's the third largest stone circle in the UK, 104m in diameter, and, bearing in mind the nearby geometric precision of Maes Howe, the only one a near-perfect circle. The Ring is related to the Neolithic settlement of Barnhouse (ca. 3300 BCE) on the matching south eastern promontory and the adjacent Stones of Stenness. Several other monuments are associated with it.

Since 2003, excavation to the immediate southeast of the Ring at the Ness of Brodgar has revealed a massive complex of monumental Neolithic buildings roughly contemporaneous with the Barnhouse settlement on a three hectare site. The substantial finds made there are still being evaluated.

Other than size, it is possibly the siting of the Ring of Brodgar that is its most significant feature. It sits on a natural raised platform on the narrow isthmus between the freshwater Loch Harray and the sea loch of Stenness within a bowl formed by Orkney's hills: Greening Hill, Skalday to the north; Mid Tooin to the northeast; Keelylang, Burrien and Wideford Hills to the east; Ward Hill, Orphir to the southeast ; Ward Hill, Hoy to the southwest and the Hill of Miffia to the west.

To stand in the centre of the Ring is to stand within two concentric circles, one natural, the other made by humans. The power of the place is palpable and gives reason to the siting of the Ring as celebration and replication of the bowl of the earth beneath the vast dome of the sky supported on those hills or on the symbolic columns of the stones.

CHECK WEBSITE FOR OPENING TIMES
NEARBY: 2 MAES HOWE

Broch of Gurness

Broch of Gurness, plan

Broch of Gurness

Aikerness, Orkney, 500–200 BCE

THE BROCH OF Gurness, walls now reduced to 3.6m high, commands a low clifftop location overlooking Eynhallow Sound with Eynhallow to the northwest and the much larger Rousay to the north. Eynhallow is from the Old Norse *Eyinhelga*, meaning holy island. It is almost impossible in Orkney to be more than a kilometre distant from some 'holy', ceremonial or ritual site. Aikerness is dotted with tumuli and chambered tombs and four further ruined brochs line the shore north of Gurness for about 4 kilometres. Brochs are unique to Scotland (some 571 have been identified, mostly in Northern Scotland and in the Northern and Western Isles). Their use is uncertain and they may have been offensive or defensive structures or demonstrative of local wealth.

Occupation of the site at Gurness is various with its original inhabitants having abandoned it by 100 CE although it was still settled until 500 CE in Pictish times and evidence of Viking burials from 900 CE has been found. The broch is circular with an open central space ca. 10m in diameter surrounded by massive four metre thick walls, gradually diminishing in thickness as they rise, which contain stairs, small chambers and stores; what came to be known as the 'inhabited wall'. The substantially complete Broch of Mousa in Shetland, on a smaller ground plan, is 13.3m high and one might suppose a similar original height at Gurness. There is evidence that brochs had at least two internal timber floors supported on timber posts and would have been roofed with timber beams possibly bearing large thin slabs of Walliwall.

CHECK WEBSITE FOR OPENING TIMES

Mediaeval: 7–18

'MEDIAEVAL', AS A CATEGORY, is imprecise and so often denotes the purely romantic: 'merrie England', the novels of Sir Walter Scott and William Morris and the works of the Pre-Raphaelite Brotherhood. However, since the buildings I have chosen range from 12th-century Romanesque to 14th-century castellated forms, some of which incorporate later Gothic and Renaissance additions of the 14th, 15th, 16th and early 17th centuries, I needed a loose parentheses. Perhaps the single formal significance of the period is the endurance of the Romanesque or Norman rounded arch in Scotland alongside, even in preference to, the pointed Gothic arch which, by the 13th century had supplanted the Romanesque elsewhere in Europe. In particular, the extended construction period for cathedrals and castles (one could argue that cathedrals are never truly completed) has them spanning centuries and different architectural idioms.

Moreover, the wars of conquest and independence that raged throughout this period seemed to require that all major constructions be fortified to provide shelter to their inhabitants whether knights, scholars, parishioners or peasants. The sturdier, plainer and more economic forms of the Romanesque were possibly better suited to this than the relatively fragile and costly stressed masonry gymnastics and decorative complexities required of the Gothic.

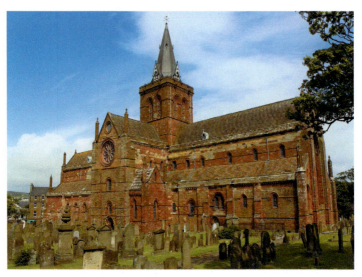

St Magnus Cathedral

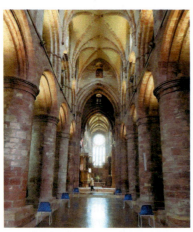

Inside St Magnus Cathedral

St Magnus Cathedral
Kirkwall, Orkney, 1137

THE BEST WAY to see St Magnus Cathedral, just as one might best experience the Campanile of St Mark's, Venice, is from the deck of a boat putting in to harbour. You might even combine it with a return journey from Balfour Castle on Shapinsay 27. The manner in which the cathedral looms over the present-day three and four-storey town is impressive but perhaps not as impressive as it would have been in comparison to the one and two-storey Kirkwall at the date of the consecration of the cathedral when the shore line was much further inland, closer to the backlands of Broad Street, roughly on the line of the present Junction Road.

Or one could follow the Norman English masons as they travelled north from Durham Cathedral, 1099–1133, to Dunfermline Abbey, 1128–50, to begin work at Kirkwall in 1137. There they assisted the Norwegians (the Orkney Isles were part of Norway until 1472 when they were gifted as recompense for an unpaid dowry) to celebrate the elevation to sainthood of Earl Magnus Erlandsson of Orkney, murdered or martyred (depending on which story you hear) on 16 April 1116 (now St Magnus day) by his betrayer, cousin and co-Earl Hakon Paulson on the isle of Egilsay.

What surprises about St Magnus Cathedral is its scale, grandeur and the sheer presence of the warm red and honey-yellow striped sandstone masonry all of which contrast spectacularly with any contemporaneous construction on mainland Scotland and, perhaps more pertinently, with those in Norway such as St Mary's Church, Bergen, ca. 1140 or Nidaros Cathedral, Trondheim, 1070–1300.

CHECK WEBSITE FOR OPENING TIMES
NEARBY: 16 TANKERNESS HOUSE

Dirleton Castle

Dirleton Castle vaults

Dirleton Castle
Dirleton, East Lothian, 1240

THE EARLIEST PARTS of Dirleton were constructed on an eminence in the village of Dirleton just west of North Berwick by the Norman-English knight John De Vaux, one among several granted lands and rights in Scotland by David I (1124–53). Subsequent owners and builders were the Haliburtons, Ruthvens and Nisbets. The effective life of the castle as residence was brought to an end by that wholesale wrecker Oliver Cromwell in 1650 as part of his occupation of Lowland Scotland during the English Civil War. The castle's location on the easy route into Scotland for English invaders had seen it damaged, sacked and rebuilt several times in 400 years. It is surrounded by a garden begun by Mary Nisbet, Lady Elgin, in the early 19th century which has had several reimaginings since, the most recent in 1993.

There are any number of Scottish castles of similar vintage, history and ruination I could have selected, so why Dirleton? It was simply the first castle I visited as a child where there was freedom to roam without intrusive educative guides or museums or collections of weapons or pots; where one's imagination had free rein and could entertain and be part of a mediaeval fantasy. It has a drawbridge, 'secret' passages, stairs hidden behind fireplaces, rooftop walks, spyholes, grand vaulted rooms, vast kitchen fireplaces and chimneys, inhabited walls, privies, guardrooms, arrowslits, inexplicable spaces and the pleasaunce of the garden. Children (and adults) can get lost in this building and in their imaginations. A proper castle.

CHECK WEBSITE FOR OPENING TIMES

Caerlaverock Castle

Caerlaverock Castle, Nithsdale Lodging

Caerlaverock Castle
Nr Dumfries, 1260–70 and 1620–34

THE ORIGINAL UNFINISHED square-planned castle of ca. 1220 built on a craig closer to the sea to control trade on the River Nith as it entered the Solway Firth was replaced by Sir Aymer Maxwell with the present moated triangular-planned construction ca. 1260. Caerlaverock is one of the very few European triangular castles and the only one in the United Kingdom. At the date of its construction and for some time later the shoreline was much closer to the castle than at present.

Caerlaverock demonstrates a very Scottish approach to economy of means and resources. European and English nobility began abandoning their castles in the early 16th century to build new Palladian palaces and houses nearby, the power of the cannon having rendered the masonry curtain-wall ineffective. In Scotland new Renaissance ranges, utilising parts of existing structure intact or as a handy quarry or supply of dressed stone, were constructed within the old castle bounds. At Caerlaverock the Nithsdale Lodging was constructed between 1620 and 1634, one of the earliest forays into Renaissance domestic architecture in Scotland. Its days were numbered, however, as the castle, housing the Catholic Nithsdales, was sacked by Protestant Covenanters in 1640, the south wall and tower substantially destroyed and the castle abandoned.

CHECK WEBSITE FOR OPENING TIMES

Lochranza Castle

Lochranza Castle
Lochranza, Arran, 13th century

IN OUTLINE, ALTHOUGH not in its detail, Lochranza has been proposed as a possible model for the castle in Hergé's Tintin adventure, *The Black Island*, first serialised in *Le Petit Vingtième* in 1937. The illustrations were updated in 1960 by Bob de Moor, Hergé's collaborator, following his visit to Portree, Skye and to Nan Eilean Siar; a recent alternative candidate is Kisimul Castle, Castlebay, Barra. As a fan of his *ligne-claire* style of comic book illustration anything with an Hergé connection has appeal to me.

Lochranza is a starker architectural, although softer landscape, counterpoint to the ubiquitous, overused and vitiated Eilean Donan, itself substantially restored in 1911, the worldwide semiotic sign for a certain sort of Scotland that's become the worldwide semiotic sign *for* Scotland. Rather than Eilean Donan's rugged island in a granite-girt sea loch, Lochranza sits on a sand spit on the north shore of Arran in the balmy Sound of Bute; another castle in another Scotland.

Extended from an earlier hall-house, L-planned Lochranza, as with any castle of its age, has been the site of significant events: Robert the Bruce's possible 1306 landing from Ireland intending to claim the throne of Scotland; Robert II's Royal hunting lodge in 1371, James IV's base in his war with the Lord of the Isles in the 1490s, Cromwell's garrison in 1650, finally to be abandoned in the later 17th century.

CHECK WEBSITE FOR OPENING TIMES

Crichton Castle

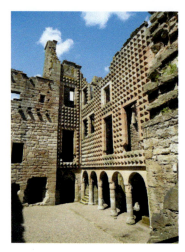

Crichton Castle, Stewart Range

Crichton Castle
Pathhead, Midlothian, late 14th century and 1590

CRICHTON CASTLE IS part of a complex including The Stables and the Collegiate Church of St Kentigern, southwest of Crichton Village. Built for the Crichton family in the late 14th, early 15th centuries, it sits in rolling moorland just above the source of the River Tyne with the Fala Moor and the Moorfoot Hills to the southeast and southwest.

This is an uncompromising structure, dominating its setting, demanding of one's attention and the traversing of a muddy 300 metre walk from the car park. If Dirleton Castle is cosy and conducive of thoughts of a colourful Arthurian mediaevalism, Crichton Castles is the unforgiving hard edge of the Middle Ages: the wars of independence, Border reiving, cruel and immediate punishment, unswerving faith, *le droit de seigneur*. However, a treasure lies within.

In the late 16th century, the then owner of Crichton, Francis Stewart, 5th Earl Bothwell, built a new lodging in the north and west ranges. The work, built ca. 1590, comprises a four-storey L plan addition. In its principal range it presents as a seven-bay arched loggia of Corinthian columns with diamond or nail-head masonry walling above. Stewart spent time in Paris and Angers and in Italy in the 1580s. What he might have seen there were the seven-bay Palazzo Pompei 1530 and Palazzo Canossa 1537 by Michele Sanmicheli and the Palazzi die Diamanti in Ferrara and Verona, the latter completed in 1582, with their diamond or nail-head façades. Crichton, in its looser organisation, is Renaissance rigour tempered by Scottish pragmatism.

CHECK WEBSITE FOR OPENING TIMES

St Machar's Cathedral

St Machar's Cathedral
Aberdeen, 14th century

ST MACHAR'S IS but a fragment of a larger whole after the central tower collapsed in a storm in 1688 taking with it the crossing, the transepts and the choir. Nevertheless, its east front is a fragment of such power and command that when Finnish architects such as Alexander Nyström, Hugo Lindberg and Armas Lindgren, significant for their creation of Finnish National Romanticism, came to Scotland in the late 19th and early 20th centuries to study granite masonry construction it featured prominently in the many subsequent reports they made to their colleagues at home.

The cathedral has had a chequered history with what we see today being the third distinct church on the site. St Machar was a companion of St Columba who, legend tells, instructed Machar to build a church where a river curves like the head of a bishop's crozier before it joins the sea. The River Don does so and the first church was begun here in 580. It was replaced by a Norman building in 1131, partly extended in the 13th century but curtailed by the Wars of Independence. The present fortified church dates from the late 14th century and is another example of the persistence of the Romanesque. The spires were added in the 15th century. There have been no bishops at St Machar's since 1690.

RESTRICTED ACCESS

Rosslyn Chapel

Rosslyn Chapel
Roslin Glen, Roslin, 1446

IT'S NOT A matter of where to begin with Rosslyn Chapel, but where to stop. An apprentice mason murdered by his jealous master; ten Sinclair Knights buried in full armour in an untraced crypt; carvings of plants from the Americas full 40 years before Columbus's arrival there; the Sinclair connections with the Zeno narrative; the Knights Templar; the location of the Holy Grail (the San Greal, the Sang Real); the incomplete Chapel part of a larger church, perhaps a copy of the Temple on the Mount, Jerusalem; Freemasonry; and so forth. Dan Brown didn't really have to try very hard, nor was he the first to respond to the hold that the Chapel has exercised on the Romantic imagination in literature and art throughout the centuries.

It was commissioned by the Norman-Scot William Sinclair, 3rd Earl of Orkney in 1446 (Orkney still part of Norway at this time). Sinclair served both the Scottish and Norwegian kings. For a while, it was thought that it had been built by Portuguese masons based on decorative similarities with the Mosteiro dos Jerónimos at Bélem although the dates (1517–72) are wrong. Present-day thinking is that the masons came from the recently completed works at Borthwick Castle. Despite this wealth of myth and misinformation, the Chapel is not diminished by it.

The Visitor Centre was designed by Page \ Park in 2012.

CHECK WEBSITE FOR OPENING TIMES

Kirbuster Farm Museum

Kirbuster Farm Museum

Kirbuster Farm Museum
Orkney, 1595 and 1723

KIRBUSTER (SOMETIMES SHOWN as Kirbister) farmhouse is tucked into a little south-facing hollow in the slope just above where the Burn of Kirbuster empties from the Loch of Houndland into the Loch of Boardhouse. Constructed, floored and roofed in Walliwall it is a long, one bay, single storey building which houses humans at one end and farm animals, piggery, barn and smiddy at the other. It is the last original unrestored 'firehoose' in Northern Europe where smoke from the fire exited the room through a timber vent in the roof (visible in the image). It even contains a stone neuk bed on the Skara Brae pattern. It is fairly representative of rural dwellings throughout Scotland even into the 20th century. According to the Listing citation of 1971 it was 'occupied until recently'. An extension at the south to create a more luxurious parlour has a lintel inscribed IS 1723 KN, the farmhouse owned by the Spence and then Hay families.

I visited it first not long after it was made into a farm museum in 1987 and got up as it must have been for much of its existence with simple furnishings and 'box-beds'. It was a blustery cool Orkney summer day outside but sat in an Orkney chair in front of the slow-burning peat fire in the huge fireplace, dying herring hung from a line above it, I was at peace. The only thing missing was a wee dram of Highland Park.

CHECK WEBSITE FOR OPENING TIMES
NEARBY: 1 SKARA BRAE

Claypotts Castle

Claypotts Castle
Claypotts Road, Dundee 16th century

WHO COULDN'T LOVE or, at least, learn to love this tiny eccentric ugly duckling of a tower house? In this view alone we have gravity-defying corbels; decorative dormer windows; caphouses eccentrically sited on the drums below which then need coping stones to protect the exposed wallheads. The gable steps back to incorporate a corbelled ledge (it's not a balcony) replete with a masonry cannon. A turnpike stair melds into the circular tower where the caphouse does not align with the central rectangular block. There are gun loops at the base, largish randomly sited 12-pane windows and smaller above.

In plan it's a Z. The Scottish tower house is modular in design comprising square, rectangular or circular accommodation towers five to seven stories in height linked by turnpike stairs resulting in L, Z, U, E and H plans, defensive in the lower floors and with varying degrees of elaboration at the highest levels. Claypotts has all that and more. The modular system permits functional planning and the subsequent expressive form; it enables the appropriate distribution of windows matched to uses within. This is architectural design of a very high order where the assembly of the parts and not the adoption of a kit of architectural decorative motives provides a logical and relatively free response to the task of housing a family.

George Gregory Smith, in *Scottish Literature: Character and Influences*, had this to say of Scottish culture which might explain Claypotts:

> …though the Scottish muse has loved reality, sometimes to maudlin affection for the commonplace, she has loved not less the airier pleasure to be found in the confusion of the senses, in the fun of things thrown topsy-turvy, in the horns of elfland and the voices of the mountains.

CHECK WEBSITE FOR OPENING TIMES

Tankerness House

Tankerness House, Orkney
Broad Street, Kirkwall, early 16th century onwards

THIS IS AN important early townhouse. Despite its having been constructed in successive phases – the north and south wings in the 1530s, the east wing and entrance arch for Gilbert Foulzie or Falzie the first post-Reformation minister of St Magnus Cathedral in 1574, the west wing for the Baikie family in 1722 and some remodelling in 1820 and conversion to museum in 1968 – it retains a consistent character of elegant urban living. The most obvious comparison is the French *maison noble*, or *hôtel*, of the 15th century constructed around a court, albeit grander with more elaborate architectural decoration, such as the House of Jacques Coeur at Bourges, 1443.

The older part presents a gable-end rather than a more conventional formal elevation to the street, a fairly common feature of Scottish urban buildings of the earlier period based around the ca. 11m wide 'burgage plots' or 'rigs' sited at right angles to the main street. For this reason inhabitants of Montrose on the Scottish mainland are known as 'gable-endies'.

Remoteness from what we presently understand to be the centres of urban and cultural sophistication – the six 'big toons' of Aberdeen, Dundee, Edinburgh, Glasgow, Inverness and Perth – has not resulted in narrow parochialism in either Orcadian ethos or building. The house contains some excellent examples of the work of Sir Stanley Cursiter (1887–1976) the renowned local artist, appointed King's Painter and Limner in Scotland in 1948.

CHECK WEBSITE FOR OPENING TIMES
NEARBY: 7 ST MAGNUS CATHEDRAL

The Study, Culross

The Study, Culross
The Cross, Culross, Fife, early 17th century

17

MY COLLEAGUE FROM Prague, Radomíra Sedláková, on seeing Culross exclaimed, 'it's just like a little toy town!' Viewers of *Outlander* may recognise it.

This almost perfectly preserved 16th-century sma burgh and trading port has little houses, narrow winding streets, a cross, an abbey, a palace and The Study. Its economy was based on the export of coal from the mine purchased from the monks of Culross Abbey by George Bruce in 1575. Bruce constructed the first undersea seam below the Forth estuary. He also set up salt-panning and cast iron manufacture. Hard to imagine such industry in Culross today. His efforts earned him a small fortune, enough to enable the construction of the palace, a knighthood and the designation of Culross as a Royal Burgh by James IV which facilitated Bruce's international trade. The flooding of the Moat mine in 1625 signalled the slow decline of Culross as a port and industrial centre.

The Study, a three storey, five-bay L-plan, is identifiable from its little caphouse. Although modernised in the lower apartments The Study contains Dutch-tiled fireplaces and, in the upper storey, oak panelling and a painted ceiling and frieze reconstructed in the 1960s to replace the original deemed beyond repair. The panelling includes the date and initials IA 1633 AP, as does a door lintel. This refers to the couple whose house it was, John Adam and Alison Primrose, and identified either the date of their marriage or their occupation of the house. This was common Scottish practice as was the retention of the wife's family name (see entries 14 and 29).

PRIVATE DWELLING

Lamb's House

Lamb's House
Water Street, Leith, Edinburgh, early 17th century

IS THIS OR is this not where Mary Queen of Scots 'remainit in Andro Lamb's hous be the space of an hour' after sailing from France in 1561, while messages were sent to Edinburgh to announce her return? There is some doubt. It may be a later house to which the name Lamb's House has stuck.

Nonetheless, Andrew Lamb was a well-connected merchant who traded with ports in France and Flanders and the present house, whatever its regal connections, represents a particularly fine example of the combined residence and warehouse of a wealthy Scottish Hanseatic or Staple merchant of the period; the crane jib and door to the attic store room partially obscured by the later balcony. The Scots propensity to extend upwards on tight plots is evident in the sculptural dormer, diminutive turnpike stair and chimney stacks. Lamb's House has equivalents throughout many North and Baltic Sea ports.

The house was remodelled in the 18th century, restored by Neil & Hurd in 1937–39 and again by Robert Hurd & Partners in 1959–61, had a brief existence as a day centre for the elderly, an even briefer period in National Trust for Scotland ownership and was bought and converted in 2010 by architects Kristin Hannesdottir and Nick Groves-Raines to create a private residence, a holiday let, an architects' office and the Icelandic Consulate. Ms Hannesdottir is Honorary Consul.

PRIVATE DWELLING

Renaissance: 19–25

THERE ARE ANY number of starting points given for the Renaissance: from Giotto's paintings in the very early 1300s to the fall of Constantinople in 1453. As an architect and perspectivist I favour the dates of Filippo Brunelleschi's experiments in perspective of 1415–20 and Leon Battista Alberti's development of it in his *Della Pittura, libri tre* of 1436.

The earliest Renaissance works in Scotland are embellishments by the Stewart kings of royal palaces at Dunfermline, Falkland, Holyrood and Linlithgow and at Edinburgh and Stirling Castles throughout the late 15th and early 16th centuries and by the wealthy landowners. It was not until Sir William Bruce's (1630–1710) use of it in his works at Holyroodhouse in the 1670s that the full gamut of the system of Classical orders – Corinthian on Ionic on Doric – made its appearance.

Although Scots architects were slow to get started with canonic Classicism, they were in full flow and highly influential throughout the late 17th and 18th centuries: Sir William Bruce and James Smith in Scotland; the Adam father and sons, William, John, Robert and James, and James Playfair throughout the United Kingdom; James Gibbs and Colen Campbell author of *Vitruvius Britannicus*, 1715–25, mostly in England and Charles Cameron in Russia.

Subsequently Neo-Classicism which made its appearance in Europe by the 1750s, employing Greek and Egyptian rather than the largely Roman models of the Renaissance as previously, can be seen in James Playfair's work, say, at Cairness House in 1791.

The Scottish Enlightenment in the middle decades of the century is also of significance in the patronage and practice of Classical architecture and its mathematical and proportional systems of organisation.

Craigievar Castle

Craigievar Castle
Alford, Aberdeenshire, 1610–26

WHILE THE NITHSDALES at Caerlaverock and Francis Stewart at Crichton built palaces within their castle walls, William Forbes, having bought his castle from the impecunious Mortimers in 1610, equally economically built his on top of its 13th-century towers, completing the pink-rendered, L-planned, seven-storey Craigievar in 1626. Forbes, known as 'Danzig Willie', reputedly made his fortune from trade with the Baltic states. Travel across the North and Baltic Seas in those times was quicker and safer than road travel generally in the British Isles. Scots historian TC Smout has recorded that part of the Danzig (Gdansk) port was known as 'Little Scotland'.

Much has been made of castles such as Craigievar – the Baronial castles – and the elaboration of their upper stories. Charles McKean considered them consistent in form and detail although not scale with French Renaissance châteaux. Other commentators, from Robert Hurd in the 1930s to Frank Walker today, have seen them as the archetypical Scottish architectural form while many others, Mansfield Forbes in the 1930s and McKean in the 1990s, have claimed them, as adapted by Charles Rennie Mackintosh, as precursors of the modernism of Le Corbusier. That's a lot of highly differentiated architectural history for a building type to carry. Let's just enjoy tower-houses such as Craigievar as did Louis I Kahn, the celebrated American architect, when he wrote of them:

> Thick, thick walls. Little openings to the enemy. Splayed inwardly to the occupant. A place to read, a place to sew... Places for the bed. For the stair... Sunlight. Fairytale.

CHECK WEBSITE FOR OPENING TIMES

Gladstone's Land

Gladstone's Land

481–3 Lawnmarket, Edinburgh 1617–21

20

IN SCOTS A 'LAND' means simply a plot within the urban plan. The original building dates from ca. 1550 and was bought in 1617 by Thomas Gledstanes and his wife Bessie Cunningham (their initials, TG BC, are carved on the skewputts). The present frontage was completed by 1621. Further additions were made in the 19th century and restorations undertaken in the 20th and, most recently, in 2021. 'Gled' is Scots for a hawk, hence the gilded hawk sculpture at the first floor.

Occupation of such tenements tended to be graded by social class with the better-off occupying the floors immediate above the shop, and the poor, the attics and cellars. This is evident in the extensive painted walls and ceilings in the lower floors and the very much plainer rooms above. The elevation presents several distinctive features of the time: the forestair to the left accessing the internal stair; the ground floor arcade or 'piazza' (a Scots misreading of an Italian plan) of which this is one of a few survivals (Elgin also has 'piazzi'); and the window arrangement of a fixed leaded light and opening timber shutters, a 20th-century restoration.

At six stories and a basement Gladstone's Land is tall although not remotely the tallest Old Town tenement where masonry construction reached heights of 13 stories and more, possibly making them the tallest residential buildings in Europe at the time and for some time subsequently. Czech playwright Karel Čapek, following his 1925 visit, wrote: 'in the old town the houses are appallingly high'.

CHECK WEBSITE FOR OPENING TIMES
NEARBY: 21 HERIOT'S HOSPITAL
45 CENTRAL LIBRARY

George Heriot's School

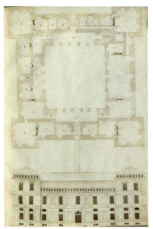

Plan by Sebastiano Serlio 1575

George Heriot's School
Lauriston Place, Edinburgh, 1628–93

Various architects

GEORGE HERIOT (D. 1624), goldsmith and moneylender to King James IV and Queen Anne, left a sum of money for the founding of a school for orphans. Heriot's Hospital was built at a time when it became more usual for Scottish architect/masons (the distinction was not yet absolute) to be identified with their works. It is thought that Heriot's nephew Walter Balcanquhall provided a 'patterne' based on a plan from Sebastiano Serlio's seventh book of architecture, first published in Frankfurt in 1575, which has also been cited as a source for Kronberg Castle, Helsingør, Denmark and the later ranges at Linlithgow Palace. While the building may be based on a late Italian Renaissance plan, the detail is Flemish which would accord with influence from Hansa and Staple trading cities there. William Wallace is the first architect/mason to be identified in the design of the building followed by William Ayton and Robert Mylne who added the tower in 1693.

George Heriot's School is a substantial departure from the Renaissance extensions and additions that preceded it, being conceived as a discrete new structure of considerable sophistication in planning and detail. It shows clearly on James Gordon's map of 1647 located on the rise to the south of Edinburgh Castle and contained with its grounds within the Telfer Wall, an extension of the Flodden Wall built in the early 1600s. A section of that wall forms the east side of Heriot Place bounding the school today.

PRIVATE SCHOOL

NEARBY: 20 GLADSTONE'S LAND
45 CENTRAL LIBRARY
100 FUTURES INSTITUTE

Inveraray

Inveraray

Inveraray, Argyll and Bute

Architects
Unbuilt plan 1747, William Adam (1689-1748)
Concept 1770, John Campbell 5th Duke of Argyll (1723-1806)
Hotel and town house, John Adam (1721-92)
Church Robert Mylne (1733-1811)

INVERARAY IS PATENTLY not a building. However, it typifies why the buildings of rural Scotland, other than a handful of survivors, do not look like those illustrated in entries 14 and 29.

Agricultural improvement in Scotland began with the 'Act anent Lands lying runrig' passed by the Scottish Parliament in 1695 whereby strip-farming was discouraged and enclosure of larger fields promoted. Improvement proceeded apace after the Act of Union with England in 1707, especially following the defeat of the Jacobite Rebellion in 1746. New villages or extensions to existing communities were constructed at Ullapool, Tobermory, Pulteneytown at Wick, Thurso and Inveraray with broad streets (wide enough to march a regiment down) and formally and symbolically sited public buildings: the barracks at Thurso and the centrally placed church framed by the townhouse and jail at the head of the main street at Inveraray. This was accompanied by the introduction of the symmetrically planned one and two-storey house or terrace found throughout the Highlands and Islands.

Inveraray is a particularly fine example of the type constructed to house the Duke of Argyll's estate workers, a woollen mill, a pier for the significant local herring fishing industry and what was to become the hotel. The architecture from the arched screen that fronts the green Avenue to residential terraces, individual houses and public buildings is consistent in appearance and of a consistently high quality. Inveraray is the archetypical 'sma burgh'.

Gunsgreen House from harbour

Gunsgreen House

Eyemouth, Berwickshire, 1753

Architect
James Adam (1732–94)

GUNSGREEN HOUSE, CREAM-RENDERED on a masonry base, commands Eyemouth harbour and is clearly visible due east from Hallydown Hill 2½ kilometres distant. It was built for the merchant and tea smuggler John Nisbet. At the time, tea was taxed at 119.5 per cent, so there was some attraction in dealing in contraband. This is a sturdy, compact, freely elevated, Classical house, designed by one of the Adam brothers, consisting of basement and three floors with *piano nobile*. It hides its secrets well in a complex plan and section complete with extensive cellars behind the buttressed fortification with its fake gun-loops (hiding in plain sight possibly), a tea chute and many concealed storage spaces. The Gunsgreen Estate was bought by Alexander Patrick in 1789 following Nisbet's bankruptcy which suggests that the excisemen, and the unpaid customs duties, had finally caught up with him.

Since 1998, after years of neglect, Gunsgreen House has been owned and restored by The Gunsgreen House Trust. The lower floors have been returned to approximately as they were in Nisbet's time with the conversion of part of the basement to form a museum/learning centre while the upper floors are holiday lets. Like Dirleton Castle this is a place to be a child in, to be a smuggler in.

CHECK WEBSITE FOR OPENING TIMES

Paxton House entrance elevation

Gateway to Paxton House

Paxton House

Nr Paxton, Berwickshire, 1757–63

Architects
House: John and James Adam
Interiors: 1773, Robert Adam (1728–92)
Gallery: 1812, Robert Reid (1770–1810)

PAXTON IS AN EXQUISITE small Adam house with an imposing Tuscan portico. It has a sad history.

Its creator Patrick Hume (1728–1808) studied at Leipzig University in 1748, moving thence to Berlin and to the court of Frederick the Great of Prussia. There he met the 18-year-old Princess Sophie De Brandt and fell in love. Obstacles were placed in the way of their union by Frederick. Dismayed but with marriage still in mind, Hume embarked on a Grand Tour only to learn while journeying in 1751 that his mother, at home in Scotland, had been murdered by a servant. Despite this tragedy he continued his tour, amassing paintings, statuary and *objets d'art* to embellish the putative marital home, returning to Scotland in 1753. He commissioned Paxton House in 1757 from the Adam Brothers as either a gift or a lure for the wedding that was never to be celebrated. Sophie, still not affianced to Hume, died in 1766. In the same year he inherited his mother's vast Wedderburn fortune and in 1771 built another grander house elsewhere.

Paxton was sold to his cousin Ninian Hume, Governor, plantation and slave-owner in Granada who had Robert Adam design the interiors funded on the Granada profits. The house then passed to George Hume who in 1812 added a gallery, designed by Reid, to house the treasures of Patrick's Grand Tour which had lain in crates unopened since his return to Scotland 60 years previously. Some of these works were subsequently sold to meet death duty obligations.

CHECK WEBSITE FOR OPENING TIMES

Stobo Castle

Biplane with folding wings

Stobo Castle
Stobo, Peebleshire, 1805–12

Architect
James Elliot (1770–1810)

THE ELLIOT BROTHERS, James and Archibald (1760–1823), sons of an Ancrum carrier and trained as joiners, ran a highly successful joint practice, James from Edinburgh and Archibald from London.

Stobo Castle, given use as a health spa in the 1970s, is a neat square-planned structure oriented northeast–southwest in the rolling hills framing Tweedale. It is constructed in an Adam castellated style with an impressive central stair and classical interior, contemporaneous with the Elliots' larger Tayport Castle. The stableyard was converted to spa use under a glazed pyramid in 1999 (by RD Cameron Associates), and a new spa building was added in 2003 (by designlab and RD Cameron). To the north of the castle is a Japanese Garden.

When the stableyard at Stobo was being converted in 1999 it was observed that, at some earlier time, its arched entrance had had two puzzling and carefully formed cut-outs, about 20 centimetres by 60 centimetres, made in the jambs either side at about 1.5 and 3.5 metres above ground level. Also, a section of stable wall had been removed and timber sliding doors substituted beneath a long steel beam. It transpired that an owner in the 1920s was accustomed to arrive at Stobo in a biplane which landed on an adjacent lawn. The biplane had wings that folded back along its sides, despite which it was still too wide to negotiate the arch and the cut-outs, at both wing heights, were made in the jambs. The biplane was stored in the adapted stables.

BOOKING REQUIRED

Revivalism: 26–47

THE PROBLEM FOR Scottish architects throughout the 19th century was the impact of unprecedented building form – factories, railway stations, exhibition halls – for which there were no historic architectural precedents other than the Roman basilica. The answer to the open-plan floors and long-span structures required of such building lay in the field of engineering. This led to much architectural speculation as to what should be the nature and appearance of an architecture appropriate to the 19th century; 'an architecture of the age'.

In Scotland, a hankering after older forms, such as had given longevity to the Romanesque, was exemplified in the interest shown in the Scotch Baronial. The impetus for this was Robert William Billings's *The Baronial and Ecclesiastical Antiquities of Scotland* published in four volumes between 1846 and 1852 which illustrated buildings of the vintage of Crichton and Craigievar Castles. The functionality of Baronialism's planning in resolving the organisation of the large country house was as important as its historic Scottish aesthetic.

Likewise, the Scottish interest in the Neo-Classical, which declined in significance elsewhere by the 1830s, continued throughout the century. The consequence of both Baronialism and Neo-Classicism, perhaps, was to demonstrate a distinctive character both in town and country not found elsewhere. Thus the twin poles of Romaticism and Rationalism were expressed in Scotland, not as in the English 'Battle of the Styles' in the diametric opposition of Classic and Gothic, but in their antinomial presence in the Baronial and Neo-Classical: Rational Romanticism and Romantic Rationalism.

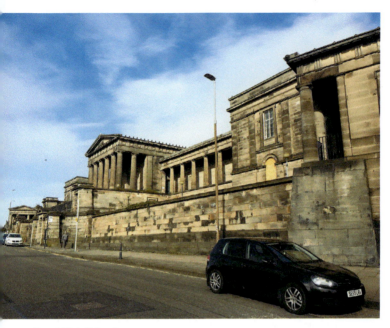

Royal High School

Royal High School
Regent Terrace, Edinburgh, 1825–9

Architect
Thomas Hamilton (1784–1858)

THE ROYAL HIGH School hugs the southwest flank of Calton Hill looking out towards the Old Town and Arthur Seat beyond. The main temple form is based on the Doric Hephaisteion in Athens but is combined in an entirely un-Doric fashion with the horizontal element of the stoa. It is piled on two layers of terrace accessed by Greek equivalents of the Egyptian Pylon or gate. The stoa terminates in pavilions also in the form of a Pylon. In its composition, it's Egyptian; in its detail, it's Greek. This is Neo-Classical architecture of a very refined sort excelled at by Scottish architects such as John Playfair, Thomas Hamilton, William Henry Playfair and Alexander Thomson. The entire ensemble acts as a Propylaea framing the incomplete replica of the Parthenon on the summit.

The school, owned by the City of Edinburgh Council, has had a chequered history since the pupils left for a new building at Barnton in 1968. First, it was destined to be the new Scottish parliament with its 'Star Trek' debating chamber. Subsequently, Edinburgh arts entrepreneur Richard Demarco secured the interest of the Thyssen-Bornemisza Collection but no financial support. Likewise, his proposal to house his unique photographic archive of post-WWII European art failed. Several developer proposals for a hotel since were thankfully refused. In 2021 the school was designated and funded as the National Centre for Music in Scotland, incorporating the Reid School of Music of the University of Edinburgh. Richard Murphy Architects and Simpson & Brown are architects for the conversion.

NO PUBLIC ACCESS

NEARBY: 58 RW FORSYTH'S
95 MURPHY HOUSE

Balfour Castle and Doocot

Balfour Castle

Shapinsay, Orkney, 1846–59

Architect
David Bryce (1803–76)

DAVID BRYCE WAS the pupil of William Burn (1789–1870) and possibly the most significant Baronial architect in Scotland. His works large and small are widespread and the architectural motives he derived and developed from those shown in Billings's books, such the crowstep or 'corbie' gable sat over an angled bay, the bay window or oriel, the square or circular attached turret, the false machicolations, the stepped string courses, among others, all of which and more are clearly evident at Balfour Castle, were reproduced throughout Scotland, even on the humblest five-storey urban tenement. The desk at which this book was written sits in such a bay window, albeit not in a Bryce house.

Balfour Castle, an extension of an earlier 17th-century house, was allegedly originally planned as a 'calendar house' – an Elizabethan architectural 'device' – with seven turrets, 12 exterior doors, 52 rooms and 365 panes of glass. The 'calendar house' is something of a rarity. There is one other in Scotland, the Neo-Classical Cairness House, 1791–91, by James Playfair, and a further eight in England. The rigour required of the client to stick to the horological demands of the architect's plan must have been taxing. And did anyone really count the number of panes?

Balfour Castle was for a while open to the public, subsequently a hotel and now appears to be a private house again.

PRIVATE DWELLING

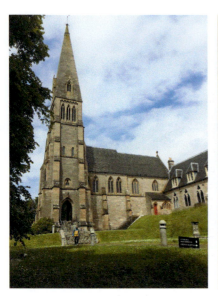
Cathedral of the Isles exterior

Cathedral of the Isles interior

Cathedral of the Isles
Millport, Great Cumbrae, 1849

Architect
William Butterfield (1814–1900)

THE INCOMPLETE SCOTTISH Episcopalian Cathedral of the Isles is tiny; it seats 80 parishioners. Unlike many Scottish Episcopalian cathedrals and churches it was not designed by Sir George Gilbert Scott although its commissioners still showed a preference for an English Gothic architect by employing William Butterfield. This was not unconnected with developments in the Anglican liturgy (with which the Scottish Episcopalians were affiliated) advanced by the Tractarians and through the patronage of the Earl of Glasgow who had been secretary of the Oxford Society for Promoting Gothic.

The Cathedral of the Isles always struck me as alien although I was unable quite to put my finger on why I thought so, that is, until I came on this passage from *Victorian Architecture* by James Stevens Curl:

Butterfield was to develop a hard, even violent and strident architecture while remaining an unrepentant Goth. His work has a strong individual character, robust and uncompromising.

The 'uncompromising' might work in the city. It certainly does at Butterfield's sensational contemporaneous polychromatic brick All Saints, Margaret Street, London, 1849–59. However, the hard edge of his Gothic Revival simply jars in the soft rolling landscape of the islands of the Firth of Clyde and in contrast to the more sympathetic rounded forms of the Romanesque and the Scottish tower house. The Cathedral of the Isles may be, in Curl's word, 'picturesque', that is, a suitable subject for a picture, but is, nonetheless, Rational rather than Romantic. The interior is quirky and colourful.

CHECK WEBSITE FOR OPENING TIMES

The Blackhouse

The Blackhouse interior

The Blackhouse

29

39 and 42 Arnol, Bragar, 1853–92
and 5a Gearrannan, Garenin, 1880s
both Isle of Lewis, Nan Eilean Siar

THE BLACKHOUSE – THE *taigh-dubh* – is the ingenious response to the challenges of limited resources, a poor economy and a severe Atlantic climate. The date of these houses which were only partially improved but occupied till the 1970s, is testament that the traditional design still worked, after a fashion. According to the Gaelic couplet:

> An iar 's anear, an dachaigh as' fhéarr
> – cùl ri gaoith, 's aghaidh rig rein.
> (East to west, the house that's best,
> back to the wind and face to the sun.)

The Blackhouse is low to the ground with rounded ends. Walls are ca. 120cm thick constructed of two leaves of fieldstone with an insulating earth core. The roof, carried on timber crucks built into the inner wall, consists of cereal thatching over turf on purlins. This is held down by a net of ropes weighted with stone. The scarcity of timber is such that the crucks are often separately owned by the clan chieftain with very strict limitations on their re-use. The entrance is located on the western side as are most of the few other openings, smoke from the open fire being removed through a vent low down in the wall. The floor is beaten earth; very occasionally stone flagged. The building is sometimes split between the *aig an teine* (living room) for the family and the *bathaich* (the byre) for their few animals.

Intrepid travellers can avail themselves of a blackhouse experience (with mod cons) a little further on from Arnol at Gearrannan.

THE BLACKHOUSE: CHECK WEBSITE
FOR OPENING TIMES.
5A GEARRANNAN: BOOKING REQUIRED
NEARBY: 3 CALANAIS STANDING STONES

Gardner's Warehouse, Jamaica Street

Gardner's Warehouse

Jamaica Street, Glasgow 1855–6

30

Architect
John Baird 1 (1798–1859)

Iron-founder
Robert McConnell (1805–67)

GARDNER'S WAREHOUSE, CONSTRUCTED only four years after Josiah Paxton's Crystal Palace for the Great Exhibition of 1851, is the oldest extant cast-iron framed and elevated building in the United Kingdom. Oriel Chambers, Liverpool followed in 1864. McConnell, the iron-founder, had been experimenting with a system of structural cast iron columns and beams since 1827 which were fully developed here. Baird's beautifully proportioned façade is based on a hugely simplified Venetian Renaissance style. In 1857–9, James Bogardus built something similar, albeit slightly taller, at Canal Street, New York.

Gardner's cast-iron Venetian Renaissance style, when it was built, was another option, alongside the many masonry revival styles, as architects struggled to find that elusive beast, 'an architecture of the age'. However, in time, it would be Baird and McConnell's structural and material vision that would prevail and cause John Ruskin, that great champion of Venetian masonry, to retreat, complaining in 1893 that:

> I perceived that this new portion of my strength had also been spent in vain; and from amidst the streets of iron, and palaces of crystal, shrank back at last to the carving of the mountain and the colour of the flower.

NO PUBLIC ACCESS ABOVE PUBLIC HOUSE

NEARBY: [40] GRECIAN CHAMBERS
[52] DAILY RECORD

Holmwood

Holmwood House cupola over stair

Holmwood

61–63 Netherlee Road, Cathcart, Glasgow, 1857–9

Architect
Alexander 'Greek' Thomson (1817–75)

THIS MAY BE the finest Neo-Classical house in Europe. I visited it first in 1991 in the company of the arch-Thomson-enthusiast the late Gavin Stamp when the house was still in use as a convent; the rooflit sideboard recess in the dining room substituting for an altar. Since then it has passed to the National Trust for Scotland and a careful programme of restoration instituted on both exterior and interior has revealed the brilliance of Thomson's architectural design and his flair as a designer of stunning interiors.

The originality of Thomson's theory and practice has had him speculated as the undocumented aesthetic link between Karl Friedrich Schinkel at the Gardener's Cottage at Potsdam, 1829–35, and Frank Lloyd Wright at the Ward Willits House, Highland Park, Chicago, Illinois, 1901. Thomson's work is emblematic of Neo-Classicism and his writings reveal his dislike of the competing Gothic. Here are his views on what he deemed as the questionable structural principles of the voussoirs in the pointed arch:

> We are all aware of the power of the wedge as a mechanical agent... What are we to think of the soundness of the mode of construction which is based upon an essentially active principle of destruction?

There was also personal affront behind this protest in that Sir George Gilbert Scott – English and a pointed-arched Goth – had been handed the commission of Glasgow University at Gilmorehill and no Scottish architect, especially Thomson, consulted.

CHECK WEBSITE FOR OPENING TIMES

St Vincent Street UP Church

St Vincent Street UP Church interior

St Vincent Street UP Church

32

265 St Vincent Street, Glasgow, 1857–9

Architect
Alexander 'Greek' Thomson

THOMSON DESIGNED THREE great churches in Glasgow and one in Edinburgh. Caledonia Road Church, 1856–7, was destroyed in an arson attack in 1965 and remains a shell. St Mary's, Edinburgh, 1858, was not built. Queen's Park UP Church, 1869, the greatest and strangest of them all, was totally destroyed in the Blitz in 1942. Only St Vincent Street UP Church, sited near the top of one of Glasgow's dunlins, remains, and not in especially great condition. The complex exterior is comprised of interpenetrating Greek forms such as at Hamilton's Royal High School, although on a much tighter ground plan. The soft Giffnock sandstone of which it is made has delaminated taking with it some of the finer incised detail. Matters are little better inside with falling plaster requiring the congregation to find other premises. The church has remained empty since 2021 which does not bode well for its future. It was recorded on the World Monuments Fund (WMF) Watchlist in 1998, 2004 and 2006. The WMF subsequently contributed to the restoration of the tower. This is a building of international significance.

Glasgow today seems neglectful of Thomson, the architect whose ubiquity established a certain *genius loci* for the city long before Mackintosh, on the strength of far fewer examples, succeeded to that status in recent times. Much of Thomson's work has disappeared or is disappearing before our eyes.

Thomson signed his buildings with a version of the Greek key motif which reads as a repeated 'T'.

NO PUBLIC ACCESS

NEARBY: 40 GRECIAN CHAMBERS
50 ST VINCENT CHAMBERS

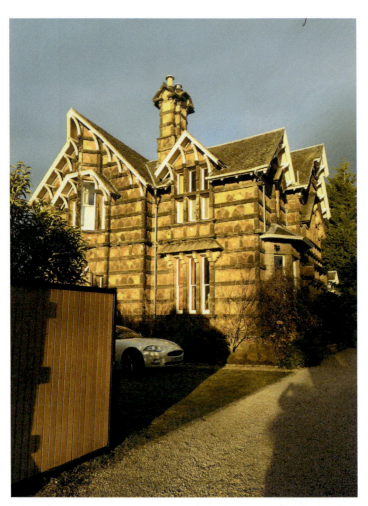

Lammerburn

Lammerburn

10 Napier Road, Edinburgh, 1860

33

Architect
(Sir) James Gowans (1821–90)

JAMES GOWANS HAD a varied career. He was, at one and the same time, architect, engineer, quarry-master, railway-builder, developer, entrepreneur and social-housing pioneer. He developed a system of modular masonry construction based on a 2ft (60cm) square, 2ft (60cm) radius circle and the angles of 22.5°, 45° and 67.5° with polygonal masonry infill in order to rationalise quarry production, reduce waste and to streamline construction on site. All these attributes are clearly identifiable at Lammerburn in both masonry and timber elements. Gowans built in this mode throughout Edinburgh, for example, at Colinton Road, ca. 1880, and in ashlar masonry construction such as at the 'Moorish' Castle Terrace tenements, 1868–70. He was knighted for his organising of the Edinburgh International Exhibition of 1886 held on the Meadows.

Gowans's work has been called 'orientalised Gothic' although his objectives were far less to do with style than with finding a new way of building economically in stone and in pinning down 'an architecture of the age'.

Gowans signed his buildings, with a stylised carved wild daisy blossom; in Scots the 'gowan'.

PRIVATE DWELLING

NEARBY: **34** BARCLAY BRUNTSFIELD
57 ST PETER'S RC CHURCH

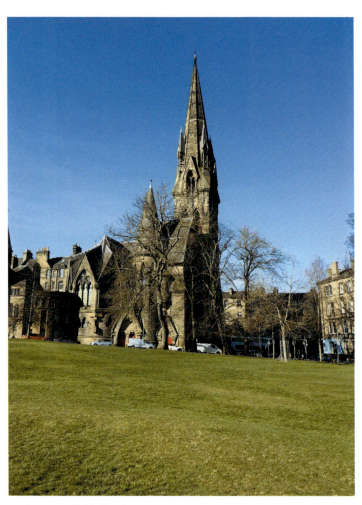

Barclay Bruntsfield Church

Barclay Bruntsfield Church

Bruntsfield Place, Edinburgh, 1861

Architect
Frederick Pilkington (1823–98)

WHILE THOMSON USED the Neo-Classical and Gowans modular masonry in the search for an 'architecture of the age', Pilkington adapted the French and Italian Gothic favoured by John Ruskin, utilised polychromatic masonry (obscured by 150 years of Edinburgh soot) and transformed the Gothic nave into a galleried, oval auditorium appropriate to the liturgy of the Free Church of Scotland. Hence the compact and truncated form of the Barclay Bruntsfield Church with great emphasis on the spire, at 250ft (80m) at the time of its completion the tallest building in Scotland and the third tallest in the United Kingdom after Norwich and Salisbury Cathedrals.

It was trunks of another sort, however, that Professor John Stuart Blackie was thinking of in 1888 when he observed, unkindly, that:

The Barclay Church was the most disorderly in the city… It looked like a congregation of elephants, rhinoceroses, and hippopotamuses with their snouts in a manger and their posteriors turned to the golf players on the [Bruntsfield] links.

Literary critic George Gregory Smith countered in *Scottish Literature: Character and Influences* that 'disorderly order is order after all'.

The dramatic interior has suffered from the domestication of the bland wallpaper that contemporary Christianity seems to prefer. Other churches by Pilkington of a similar format are to be found at Irvine, Kelso and Penicuik.

RESTRICTED ACCESS
NEARBY: 33 LAMMERBURN
57 ST PETER'S RC CHURCH

Wallace Monument

Wallace Monument

Abbey Craig, nr Stirling, 1862

Architect
John Rochead (1814–78)

IN SCOTLAND WE celebrate our heroes often and generously. Robert Burns, who spoke for Scots folk, has 27 monuments dotted around the country. Sir Walter Scott, who wrote about the Scottish nation for the world, has his monument in Edinburgh, his tomb in the ruins of Dryburgh Abbey and his house at Abbotsford. William Wallace, who fought for Scottish independence, has monuments at Ayr, Aberdeen, Paisley, Bemersyde (nr. Melrose) and at Stirling.

The monument commemorates Wallace as a significant, although losing, champion of Scotland in the 13th and early 14th centuries. It was funded by public subscription and foreign donation, including from Italian patriot Guiseppe Garibaldi. It was won in competition by Rochead in 1858. He had already received favourable attention for his Scots Baronial City of Glasgow Bank in Trongate, Glasgow, 1855. The bank is merely picturesque, however, when compared to the Monument's 220 feet (67m) of uncompromising ruggedness and toughness sat on the 340 feet (111m) of Abbey Craig. Outside and in it is constructed from rock-faced rubble masonry with ashlar dressings and mouldings and utilises every dramatic motif that Rochead could hoover up from the pages of Billings's *Baronial and Ecclesiastical Antiquities of Scotland,* all topped with a crown spire based on that of St Giles' Cathedral in Edinburgh.

There are spectacular views of the Forth valley and Stirling Castle from the platform at the very top. Be warned, that's 220 feet (67m) of spiral stair, there is no lift.

CHECK WEBSITE FOR OPENING TIMES

Kibble Palace

Kibble Palace interior

Kibble Palace

Botanic Gardens, Glasgow, 1863–73

Designer
John Kibble (1815–94)

TODAY WE MARVEL at the computer's facility to generate and meld thousands of individually shaped and sized two-dimensionally curved construction components into non-rectilinear buildings of complex form. This is known as 'parametric' design. One hundred and fifty years ago, with nothing more sophisticated to hand than a wooden drawing board, tee-square, set square and compasses, his own imagination and the skill of the craftspersons employed, John Kibble created this beautiful translucent and parametrical greenhouse. Originally erected at his house at Coulport on Loch Long in 1863–6, it was transported to the Botanic Gardens and with the assistance of architects James Boucher and James Cousland and iron-founder John Boyd of Paisley, re-erected and extended in 1873. In addition to the ingenuity of its form it contains a lush collection of exotic tree-ferns and houses several fine sculpture groups; very nearly the *gesamtkunstwerk*.

Kibble, son of a steel stockholder, was a Victorian eccentric and entrepreneur who invented a bicycle that could travel on water and 'cycled' it across Loch Long. He was an enthusiastic photographer exhibiting in Aberdeen, Glasgow and Edinburgh in the 1850s, an early adopter, in 1853, of the collodion wet-plate process, invented 1848–51, which due to the rapidity of the process required a mobile darkroom. In 1858 Kibble constructed the then largest camera in the world with a 13 inch (33cm) lens which had to be transported by means of a horse and cart.

The Kibble was completely restored in 2006.

CHECK WEBSITE FOR OPENING TIMES
NEARBY: 87 21ST CENTURY TENEMENT

Fountainbridge tenement

Fountainbridge tenement

158–164 Fountainbridge, 90–92 Grove Street Edinburgh, 1864

Architect
Frederick Pilkington

POOR OLD FREDERICK Pilkington. He seemed yet again to have upset the architectural press. The anonymous editorial writer of *The Builder* of 18 February, 1865 had this to say:

> The sensational mania has spread from our literature to our architecture; an example of this is to be seen in Grove-street, the work of Mr Frederick Pilkington. In a given space the architect seems to have striven to produce every variety of window; the pointed arch, round arch, elliptical arch, and horse-shoe arch, are in juxtaposition – the whole being decorated with a profusion of carving of natural foliage: repose for the eye there is none and an uncanny effect is produced upon the spectator. It is with considerable regret we make these observations as a step in this direction was much needed to relieve the dreary monotony of the west-end architecture, but Mr Pilkington has outrun prudence. With less effort after novelty, and more attention to elegance of proportion and harmony of effect, Mr Pilkington may yet do something more worthy of commendation.

How tastes change. On one point *only* do I agree with the writer in *The Builder*. The Fountainbridge tenement does much 'to relieve the dreary monotony of west-end architecture' currently being erected nearby.

PRIVATE DWELLING OVER SHOPS
NEARBY: 76 TELEPHONE EXCHANGE

National Museum of Scotland, main hall

National Museum of Scotland
Chambers Street, Edinburgh, 1864

Architect
Captain Francis Fowke (1823–65)

MY MOTHER FIRST took me to the National Museum of Scotland (formerly the Royal Museum of Scotland) when I was 5 years old to see the Egyptian mummies. It presented then, in the early 1950s, much as I guess it had in the 19th century when taxonomy was the thing and exhibits reeked of catalogues, academism, formal study and formaldehyde. More engaging display and information, not didacticism, had to wait on the 1970s. That first visit and the effect on me of the main hall was to determine the course of my life. In that moment, however inchoate, I understood the power of architecture. Even today, Fowke's massive dour and blackened Lombardic Renaissance exterior does not prepare the visitor for the lightness and gaiety of the white filigree confection of the interior.

Fowke followed in a tradition of military men (he was commissioned in the Royal Engineers) acquiring perforce architectural training and experience in the conduct of their military duties which led to significant public commissions, such as the Royal Albert Hall and V&A in London, where his knowledge of cast iron construction facilitated those large spaces the age demanded.

Recent reinvention of the Museum has seen galleries and treasures come and go: the repatriation of indigenous peoples' significant cultural artefacts; and the clearer understanding of the role of Empire in acquisition. The substantial reconfiguration and modernisation of the Museum 2011–16 was designed by Hoskins Architects.

CHECK WEBSITE FOR OPENING TIMES
NEARBY: 20 GLADSTONE'S LAND
45 CENTRAL LIBRARY
89 MUSEUM OF SCOTLAND
100 FUTURES INSTITUTE

The McManus

The McManus: Dundee's Art Gallery and Museum

Albert Square, Dundee, 1865

Architect
Sir George Gilbert Scott (1811–78)

IT IS SOMETIMES forgotten that Dundee has a gallery other than the V&A with a superb collection of works celebrating Dundee and its talented people. Originally called the Albert Institute, the largest memorial to Queen Victoria's Prince Consort outside London, it has been renamed, in less royalist times, for a noted Lord Provost.

Scott, from his *Personal and Professional Recollections* published posthumously in 1879, unintentionally describes how arcane 19th-century architectural revivalism could be in the search for an 'architecture of the age'. He began not in Dundee but in Hamburg with his winning but unbuilt 1855 entry for the Rathaus competition on which, according to Historic Environment Scotland, the McManus is based.

I founded my design [for the Rathaus]... upon the Halle at Ypres, but changed the detail entirely... I was commissioned to erect the new University buildings at Glasgow, a very large work, for which I adopted a style which I may call my own invention, having already initiated it in the Albert Institute at Dundee. It is simply a 13th or 14th century secular style with the addition of certain Scottish features peculiar in that country to the 16th century though in reality derived from the French style of the 13th and 14th centuries.

Upgrading was undertaken to designs by Page \ Park in 2005.

CHECK WEBSITE FOR OPENING TIMES
NEARBY: 86 DUNDEE REP
90 DCA
97 V&A DUNDEE

Grecian Chambers

Grecian Chambers

336–356 Sauchiehall Street, Glasgow, 1865

Architect
Alexander 'Greek' Thomson

GRECIAN CHAMBERS, ALTHOUGH lacking some care, is a stunning prospect and reveals clearly the evolution of the several strands of Thomson's practical and theoretical interpretation of the Neo-Classical and its Greek and Egyptian roots. Practicality is exemplified by the regularity, economy and rigour of the cast iron framed construction and in the democracy of the fenestration, while theory is represented by a number of guiding principles in architectural design he got from *Essays on the Nature and Principles of Taste* by the Scottish Episcopalian priest and essayist Archibald Alison. This required that the column should appear appropriate in scale to the load it bore. The second principle concerned the potential of infinite horizontal extension implied in Greek and particularly Egyptian architecture. Both principles are evident here.

The detail of the columns, capital, architrave and entablature are Thomson's own developed from Greek and Egyptian precedent but wholly transformed into something new. Also a Thomson trademark is the near total disengagement of the top floor windows from the adjacent columns. This is urban commercial architecture of unique quality and points to the architectural and constructional developments in such buildings in the 1880s and beyond. Recent Scottish Government funding will facilitate refurbishment of the Centre for Contemporary Arts located on the ground floor.

NO PUBLIC ACCESS OVER SHOPS

NEARBY: 32 ST VINCENT ST. CHURCH
50 ST VINCENT CHAMBERS
54 WILLOW TEA ROOMS
56 LION CHAMBERS

Mortuary Chapel, Western Cemetery

Mortuary Chapel
Western Cemetery, Arbroath, 1875

Designer
Patrick Allan-Fraser (1813–90)

NO ONE VIEWPOINT outside or in can encompass the totality of this extraordinary building, a fantastic mash-up of every detail from Robert Billings's *Baronial and Ecclesiastical Architecture of Scotland* and more. Rosslyn Chapel seems restful in comparison.

Patrick Allan from Arbroath had an unsettled early career, never quite finding his métier until enrolling at the Trustees' Academy in Edinburgh to study art. This was followed by time in Rome, Paris and London in the 1830s, Allan only returning to Arbroath in 1842 in the hopes of illustrating an edition of Sir Walter Scott's *The Antiquary*. This was never proceeded with. However, Allan met and married the reasonably well-off widow Elizabeth Fraser and set about restoring her estates. Elizabeth's mother died in 1851, her bequest substantially increasing their income, and Allan was able to further indulge his tastes as a self-taught architect in more substantial works on the several large houses and grounds they now owned. Allan was not shy in expressing his views on architecture which were published in an article entitled 'Amateur Criticism of Architectural Works' in *The Building Chronicle* of May 1854.

Elizabeth died in 1873; the Mortuary Chapel is dedicated to her memory. From this time Allan used Fraser-Allan as his family name. Their greatest benefaction was the Patrick Allan Baronialised Hospitalfield House, Arbroath, which became and remains a residential centre for staff and students of the Scottish Art Colleges.

CHECK WEBSITE FOR OPENING TIMES

Queen's Cross Church

Queen's Cross Church

Queen's Cross, Aberdeen, 1879–81

Architects
John Bridgeford Pirie (1848–92)
and Arthur Clyne (1853–1924)

ASCRIBING AN ARCHITECTURAL style to this church has always seemed problematic. Historic Environment Scotland describe it as 'Rogue-Gothic'. This would align Pirie and Clyne's design alongside those of revival architects such as Teulon and Keeling in England who were known to have taken considerable liberties in their interpretation of Gothic. Fiona Sinclair, in 1984, saw 'proto-Secessionist' detailing in parts of the Church, where, in the 1890s, Finnish architects (see also 12) had taken inspiration from it in their creation of Finnish National Romanticism, a Freestyle associated with Art Nouveau and Jugendstil.

Does this really matter? Did it matter when tracing George Gilbert Scott's convoluted route to arrive at a style 'that [he] might call [his] own invention'? Perhaps it does. Pirie and Clyne refrained from over-working the Kemnay granite as a strict observance of Gothic decorative practice might have demanded and, in a manner that became commonplace in the 20th century, allowed the nature and quality of the material itself to resonate with minimal carving. It was this aspect that the Finns saw, understood and transformed. So, I'm inclined to go with Sinclair and the Finns and to see this beautifully crafted building as *proto*-Secessionist; a hint of what's to come. That's why it's here and not in the *Début de siècle* section. Judge for yourself.

RESTRICTED ACCESS

NEARBY: 44 JOHN MORGAN HOUSE

St Conan's Church, Lochawe

Nave and chancel St Conan's Kirk

43 St Conan's Kirk

Lochawe, Argyll and Bute, 1881–6 and 1907–30

Designer
Walter Douglas Campbell, (1850–1914)

WALTER DOUGLAS CAMPBELL was an amateur architect who appeared to have sufficient private wealth (like Patrick Allan) that enabled him to realise a private fantasy. He bought the island of Innis Chonain where the River Awe empties into the loch and built a 'stately mansion-house' for his sister Helen, his mother, Mrs Caroline Campbell, and himself. Google maps today show the outline of a large structure, now gone – presumably the remains of the house – within which stands a mid-20th-century dwelling.

Mrs Campbell seemingly found the journey to nearby Dalmally for Sunday worship tiresome so Campbell acquired the existing parish church in Lochawe, much closer to Innis Chonain, and substantially extended it. He was a collector of antiquarian artefacts and a re-purposer of salvaged material. Arcading and some masonry in the church came from the Reformed Church in Inchinnan while timber was retrieved from the scrapped former battleships *Caledonia* and *Duke of Wellington* for use in the roofs and doors. The church is designed in a very free Romanesque and Norman style but with elements drawn from a variety of other sources. After Campbell's death, the Church was completed by the family although it was not consecrated until 1930 long after it was of any practical use to Mrs Campbell. Like the Mortuary Chapel at Arbroath, St Conan's has an exuberance and license the formally trained architect might baulk at but the fact that it speaks of joy in a dream made solid rather than the correct observance of a canon is what appeals.

RESTRICTED ACCESS

50 Queen's Road

John Morgan House

50 Queen's Road, Aberdeen, 1885

44

Architects
John Bridgeford Pirie and Arthur Clyne with John Morgan

BY 1877, JOHN MORGAN (1844–1907) ran one of the principal construction companies in Aberdeen, Adam Mitchell & Co., which he had inherited from his uncle. Significant works undertaken were the extension to Marischal College, the Northern Assurance Offices and Canada House. They exported granite dressings to London, Liverpool, New York, Toronto and Sydney.

Morgan's education was limited and he was largely self-taught, what we would know in Scotland as a 'lad o' pairts'. Voracious reading and the creation of a substantial private library provided the intellectual heft for his membership of the Aberdeen Senate (a debating club), the Aberdeen Philosophical Society to which he gave papers on John Ruskin, founding membership as a Companion of John Ruskin's Guild of St George and founding membership of the Ruskin Society of Aberdeen. He was a correspondent of both Ruskin and Thomas Carlyle.

50 Queen's Road, designed jointly by Morgan and Pirie, has been characterised as a builder's advertisement, overburdened with impeccably laid masonry and impressively carved but restless detail; Rogue-Gothic, according to Historic Environment Scotland. It's perhaps rather more than that with hints of Alexander Thomson (entries 32 and 40), with whom Pirie had a connection through his mentor Robert Gordon Wilson, and of the American architect Henry Hobson Richardson (1838–86). A nearby development of houses for Morgan in Hamilton Place by Pirie and Clyne exhibit a more controlled version of the Queen's Road aesthetic. Pirie resided at number 26.

PRIVATE DWELLING

NEARBY: 42 QUEEN'S CROSS CHURCH

Central Library

Central Library
George IV Bridge, Edinburgh 1887–90 and 1901–3

Architect
Sir George Washington Browne
(1853–1939)

Depending on how you define 'public', the oldest public library in Scotland is at Innerpeffray Chapel, Crieff where, in 1690, the Drummonds permitted public access to the family library or at Kirkwall founded in 1693 with a gift of 150 books from William Baikie. Two hundred years were to elapse before Edinburgh followed suit.

Edinburgh could boast, in an 1849 report, of 219 books for every 100 inhabitants compared to a mere 24.5 for every 100 in London. However, these books were all in *private* libraries. The Public Libraries Act of 1850 which permitted the financing of libraries from the rates did not inspire the City Council nor did the Library Association of the United Kingdom's third annual meeting held in Edinburgh ca. 1880.

It took a gift of £50,000 from Andrew Carnegie in 1886, to get the ball rolling.

The subsequent architectural competition was won by Browne under the pseudonym 'Bibliotheque'. His design is an ingenious Greek cross dressed up in a lavish Francois Premier revival style inside and out.

The Central Library is by far the best place to study in Edinburgh and many happy hours have been spent in the Scottish Room and Fine Art Library. Be warned, however, there is a very limited lift access and accommodation is situated over eight floors.

CHECK WEBSITE FOR OPENING TIMES.

NEARBY: 20 GLADSTONE'S LAND
21 HERIOT'S HOSPITAL
38 NATIONAL MUSEUM
64 NATIONAL WAR MEMORIAL
89 MUSEUM OF SCOTLAND
100 FUTURES INSTITUTE

Templeton's

Templeton's detail

Templeton's Carpet Factory

62 Templeton Street, Glasgow, 1889 and 1936

Architects
William Leiper (1839–1916)
George Boswell (1879–1952)

THIS IS POSSIBLY the most colourful and mobile corner in Scotland if something of a car-crash junction of towers. To the left is William Leiper's richly modelled, and not a little strident, homage to Venetian Gothic in red brick with a coloured panel below the corbel table at the eaves representing a carpet pattern. To the right is Boswell's extension, a seemingly functionalist response to the factory brief, which he has topped with an attic and parapet in coloured tiles that trumps even Leiper's polychromatic excess. Each building turns the corner in a fashion appropriate to its age: Leiper's with a projecting tower containing a turnpike stair (the rising, spiralling windows the giveaway); Boswell's in a tight expressionistic polished black granite quarter-drum with curved horizontally glazed windows set back behind the brick flanking walls.

Both parts are transcendent in their own way. Leiper by using Ruskin's Venetian polychromy has escaped Ruskin's strictures on commercial architecture; Boswell by the identical use of colour has escaped the tedium of the modernist factory anticipated with dread by Ruskin. It's often been remarked that buildings have a limited capacity to express emotion. Templeton's is the refutation of the view. Here is joy, exuberance, pride in product and the broadcasting of it to the world.

In 1985 the building was converted to a business centre.

NO PUBLIC ACCESS

NEARBY: 92 HOMES FOR THE FUTURE

Kirkton Cottages

Kirkton Cottages

1, 2 & 3 Kirkton Cottages, Fortingall, Perth and Kinross, 1889–93

47

Architect
James Marjoribanks MacLaren
(1853–90)

BETWEEN 1874 AND 1904, the several *Sketchbooks* published by the Edinburgh Architectural Association and the Glasgow Institute of Architects together with MacGibbon & Ross's detailed and measured survey, *The Castellated and Domestic Architecture of Scotland from the 12th to the 18th Centuries*, published 1887, provided Scottish architects with more accurate information than had Billings's volumes previously. MacLaren, a sketcher, was perhaps the precursor of Charles Rennie Mackintosh and Robert Lorimer (MacLaren's pupil) in his interpretation of these traditional models. His practice, based in London, had projects in Las Palmas, Cornwall and throughout the southeast of England. In Scotland, he designed the extension to Stirling High School, 1887 (which he had attended as a child), the tower of which was copied by Mackintosh at the Glasgow Herald Building, 1893–4, and for the Glen Lyon Estates at Fortingall from 1886. Tragically, in 1890 at the age of 37 he succumbed to tuberculosis. Kirkton was completed by Dunn & Watson (his partner) in 1893.

This little corner demonstrates how manipulation of the parts of a gable end – flue, windows, entrance, flanking walls – were to become of significance to Scottish Art Nouveau architects in the succeeding decade.

As a very minor footnote, in 2015, I designed the subdivision into flats of MacLaren's first independent commission, then lying empty and vandalised, Avon Hall in Grangemouth, built 1877 for his cousin.

PRIVATE DWELLING

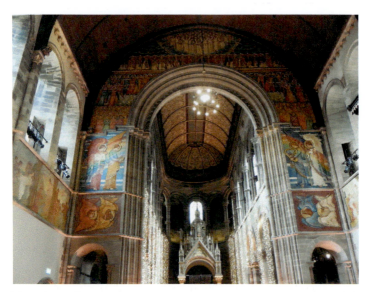

Traquair murals

Mansfield Traquair Centre
Mansfield Place, Edinburgh, 1872–85 and 1893–1901

Architect
Church, Robert Rowand Anderson (1834–1921)
Artist, interior, Phoebe Anna Traquair (1852–1936)

THE MANSFIELD TRAQUAIR Centre is a large solid Norman Revival building by Robert Rowand Anderson. However, its triumph is the mural and ceiling paintings by the Irish-born Phoebe Anna Traquair who settled in Edinburgh in 1874. Her first mural commission, revealing the influence of William Blake, Dante Gabriel Rossetti and John Ruskin on her work, was the decoration of the Mortuary Chapel at the Hospital for Sick Children, Sciennes, Edinburgh, 1885–6. Her work at St Mary's Cathedral, Palmerston Place, Edinburgh, 1888–92, brought her international recognition while the Mansfield Church, begun 1893, is her magnum opus, sometimes referred to as 'Edinburgh's Sistine Chapel'.

Originally the Catholic Apostolic Church, it was the creation of the Church of Scotland Minister Edward Irving and had a liturgy drawn from the Protestant, Roman Catholic and Greek Orthodox traditions reflected in the murals which in both time and in style are a bridge between late 19th-century Arts & Crafts and early 20th-century Art Nouveau. They are the eastern Scottish counterpart to the contemporaneous work of the Glasgow School and Mackintosh, McNair and the MacDonald sisters.

Further paintings by Traquair are at the National Gallery of Scotland at the Mound and her decorative and hand-crafted work at the National Museum of Scotland, Chambers Street (38).

BOOKING REQUIRED
NEARBY: 26 ROYAL HIGH SCHOOL
58 RW FORSYTH'S
66 ST ANDREW'S HOUSE
95 MURPHY HOUSE

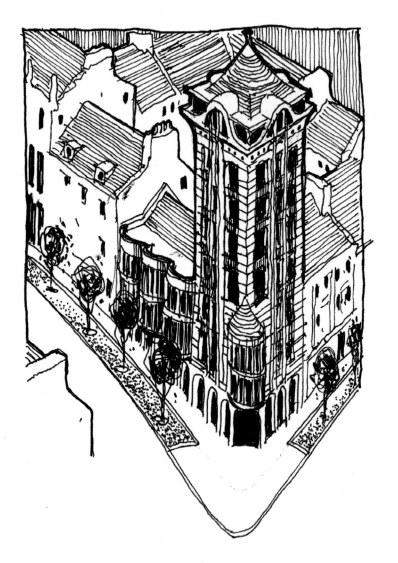

Début de siècle: 49–63

EVERYONE KNOWS THE term l'Art Nouveau. It is often employed as a catch-all to describe what was happening throughout European avant-garde architecture, art and design when *fin de siècle* became *début de siècle* and thoughts turned to the dawning century in the years 1890 to 1910. L'Art Nouveau was less a matter of *a* style than it was that of several related styles. Each professed novelty and employed stylised, even abstracted, human and botanical models; adaptations of the earlier Revival styles; the art of Japan and the products of local ethnographic or historic building surveys conducted in the late 19th century.

In Scotland we have no unique name for it. It is associated most often with the work of Charles Rennie Mackintosh, Margaret MacDonald Mackintosh, Herbert McNair and Frances MacDonald McNair – 'The Four' as they were known – and with the work of James Salmon, EA Walton, the Glasgow School and the Glasgow Girls. There are, however, discrete characteristics present in Scottish Art Nouveau which differentiate it from its continental counterparts. Even in the most exuberant examples, such as in some of the designs of Salmon, Scottish Art Nouveau designers show a preference for a more rectilinear almost Neo-Classical expression which is combined with the flattened perspective of Japanese art. If such was the avant-garde preference in the west, a refined Arts & Crafts was its eastern variant in the work of Robert Lorimer, Hunter Crawford and Matt Steele and others where the influence of the English designers WR Lethaby and CFA Voysey was more prominent.

A more sympathetic interpretation of Scottish traditional architecture also remained of significance east and west as did the Revival styles. The Renaissance revival morphed into a powerful commercial Baroque accompanied with constructional experimentation.

Melsetter House

Melsetter House
Hoy, Orkney 1898–1900

49

Architect
William Richard Lethaby (1857–1931)

a sort of fairy palace on the edge of the great northern seas... a very loveable place... built for home life as well as for dignity.

SO SAID MAY Morris, William Morris's daughter. Melsetter is an early 18th-century house altered and extended by William Richard Lethaby, the English architect and architectural historian for the Birmingham industrialist Thomas Middlemore and his wife Theodosia, May Morris's friend, and who had Caithness ancestry. Lethaby was the author of *Architecture, Mysticism and Myth* of 1891 which influenced Arts & Crafts and Art Nouveau designers in the United Kingdom. Mackintosh quoted large parts of it in his lecture 'Architecture' he gave at Glasgow in 1893.

The sharp-eyed reader will have noticed that Melsetter is not made from Walliwall. Hoy's local sandstone is reddish and laid down in much thicker bedding-planes, hence the more regular size of the ashlar blocks. It is thought that Lethaby may have acted rather as a Mediaeval master mason directing design and construction as near-simultaneous processes, relying on the inherent skills and flexibility of the local masons to bring the house to fruition. He may have learned the very English Free-Style triple gable from his friend Philip Webb, William Morris's architect. In a version of the celebratory lintel, Lethaby has had Thomas and Theodosia's initials carved on the gable, omitting the initial of Theodosia's family name as was the English custom.

Lethaby also worked on several adjacent estate buildings. His imprint is obvious.

BOOKING REQUIRED

The Hatrack, St Vincent St

St Vincent Chambers (The Hatrack)   50
St Vincent Street, Glasgow, 1899–1902

Architect
James Salmon (1873–1924) of Salmon, Son & Gillespie

OF ALL THE Scottish Art Nouveau designers, the early work of James Salmon most nearly approached that of the Europeans. In 'The Hatrack' façade (so named for its spiky protuberances) the slender sculptural and architectural elements elide from one to another presenting neither as sculpture nor architecture and compare closely with Gaudí's later Casa Milá, Barcelona, 1906. There is extensive Art Nouveau metalwork at the stair and lift shaft. Such was Salmon's European context – he had travelled to Pisa, Venice and Lucerne in the early 1890s – that the French magazine *L'Art Decoratif* included a long article on his work in an issue of 1899. Nevertheless, there is order in this façade and Raymond O'Donnell, Salmon's biographer, was to note of the practice at this time that, 'a growing rationality had begun to develop in their work'.

Salmon's choice of elevational treatment at The Hatrack was not entirely aesthetic as the narrow deep-plan site required maximum daylight to penetrate its depths; there are also light wells within the building. The lightness of the façade masonry and the extent of glazing was made possible by a hidden steel frame behind the masonry to support its weight. Salmon's elevation design, as it sits between a contemporaneous Renaissance Revival mass masonry frontage to the right, its antecedent, and the glum 1980s glass and steel to the left, its inelegant inheritor, was to be realised more fully in the early curtain walls of the 1930s.

NO PUBLIC ACCESS

NEARBY: 32 ST VINCENT ST. CHURCH
40 GRECIAN CHAMBERS
54 WILLOW TEA ROOMS
56 LION CHAMBERS

Hill House gable

Hill House

8 Colquhoun Street Upper, Helensburgh 1902–04

Architect
Charles Rennie Mackintosh
(1868–1928)

BOOKS HAVE BEEN written about this remarkable house and it appears in every history of modern architecture. What little I want to add is detail.

Mackintosh disaggregated a typical Scottish end gable into its constituent parts – the two chimney stacks large and small, the entrance, the partial oriel window and rearwards extension of the stair tower – and either recessed or projected them in an Expressionist manner from the flat plane of the wall (see also entry 47). He developed this motif further in the end gable of his roughly contemporaneous competition entry for the House for an Art Lover (see entry 88). The celebrated architectural historian Nikolas Pevsner made this connection:

From here a direct way leads to that peculiar and short-lived Expressionism in Continental and especially Dutch architecture…

Readers from the Netherlands might like to compare the roughly contemporaneous works of Michel de Klerk or Piet Kramer with the Hill House gable and with Craigievar.

Unwisely, Mackintosh dispensed with copes and rendered Hill House in Portland cement rather than traditional hygroscopic lime harling which has led to a century's-worth of water-retention in the walls. It is currently shrouded in a vast tent while it dries out. This has had the benefit of allowing the installation of high level viewing balconies.

CHECK WEBSITE FOR OPENING TIMES

Daily Record Building

Daily Record Printing Works

Renfield Lane, Glasgow, 1900–4

52

Architect
Charles Rennie Mackintosh

THE GLASGOW GRID matches the main east–west streets with parallel narrow service lanes that bisect the city blocks. The Daily Record Printing Works is located on such a lane which makes it tricky to photograph and only a little easier to see. Nevertheless, the sheer joy and exuberance of the façade in a gloomy urban canyon is more than compensation for a crick in the neck.

Mackintosh recognised the challenge of its location and designed a frontage, over a sandstone base and under a sandstone attic, in predominantly white glazed brick with multi-coloured glazed bricks representing either the Tree of Knowledge, Tree of Life or simply the origin of the paper on which the news was printed.

Mackintosh's early Symbolist background, as evidenced in his watercolours, such as *The Tree of Personal Effort* and *The Tree of Influence*, both 1895, is of significance when reading the decorative imagery he employed in his architecture. Of all his works, together with the elevation of the Willow Tea Rooms, Sauchiehall Street, the Daily Record compares most directly with European Jugendstil or Sezession decoration of designs such as Josef Hoffmann's Purkersdorf Sanatorium, near Vienna, of 1905, or Bruno Taut's commercial building at Kottbusser Damm, Berlin, of 1910.

There is a café/bar on the ground floor.

NO PUBLIC ACCESS ABOVE CAFE
NEARBY: 30 GARDNER'S WAREHOUSE
98 QUEEN STREET STATION

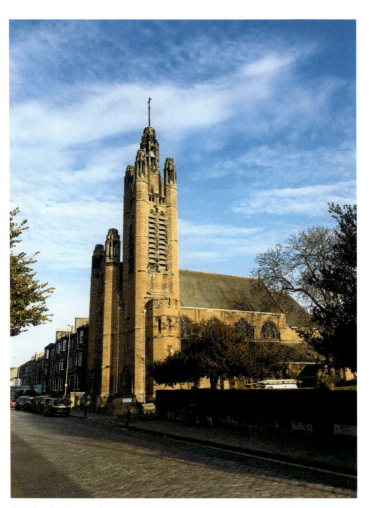

St John the Evangelist

St John the Evangelist RC Church
35 Brighton Place, Portobello, Edinburgh, 1903–06

Architect
James Thomas Walford (1832–1908)

EDINBURGH HAS VERY few canonic Art Nouveau buildings, the Arts & Crafts being the east coast preference, and it might be stretching the point to describe St John's as Art Nouveau. In defence, the overall Rogue-Gothic exterior – the interior is entirely Gothic – has been subtly modified by the non-Gothic convex caps to the pinnacles and convex tracery in some of the windows The main tower and open-work pinnacles show a generic similarity to the contemporaneous works of the English Free-Style architect ES Prior and, in the detail, to the towers on the transepts of Mackintosh's Liverpool Cathedral competition entry of 1903. I appreciate this kind of analysis can be readily dismissed as trainspotting.

Nonetheless, it's a puzzling building, being the rather adventurous and youthful late composition by a London architect with an otherwise unremarkable and unmarked career – a solitary pleasant but conventional Arts & Crafts Tudor house in Taplow is illustrated in *The Builder* of 28 September 1885. St John's was undertaken, possibly for no fee, very late on in his life when he was resident, either permanently or in a holiday house, in Joppa Road, Portobello where he died. The answer must lie in Walford's otherwise silent biography. Was the church design offered in thanks or in exculpation for a significant life event? Are there other, as yet unidentified, works by Walford that might explain St John's?

RESTRICTED ACCESS

Willow Tea Rooms

Willow Tea Rooms

217 Sauchiehall Street, Glasgow, 1903

Architect
Charles Rennie Mackintosh

MOST COMMENTARY ON this building focuses, rightly, on the spectacular interior and you must take tea there when in Glasgow. However, the plainer elevation permits some further thoughts on the derivation of the rectilinearity of Scottish Art Nouveau.

The *sauch* of Sauchiehall Street is the Scots word for willow, hence the significance of Miss Catherine Cranston's choice of the name for her tea room, which was one of her chain of tea rooms intended to wean the Glaswegian off strong drink. The willow as symbol most often represents strength and endurance, which might have been required by Miss Cranston in her quest, and wisdom, maturity and healing which last was no doubt her objective. In Celtic mythology the willow represents good luck and touching a willow is the origin of the custom to 'knock on wood'.

The building is the adaptation of an existing four-storey tenement which has been given a new façade and interior. The depth of the window returns in the top floors emphasises the presence of the 'inhabited' wall of Baronial origin while Celtic influence is present in the jewel-like geometric shopfront and first floor window. Finally, contact with the designers and artists of the Weiner Sezession have influenced the whiteness of the façade and the inclusion of the shared motives of the coloured tile and painted punctuation of the ground floor window spandrel, the upper floor window soffits and the eaves verge.

CHECK WEBSITE FOR OPENING TIMES
NEARBY: 32 ST VINCENT ST. CHURCH
40 GRECIAN CHAMBERS
50 ST VINCENT CHAMBERS
56 LION CHAMBERS

Riselaw House

Riselaw House
53 Pentland Terrace, Edinburgh, 1904

55

Architects
John Graham Gordon (1875–?)
Bennet Dobson (1871–?)

ALTHOUGH MANY OF the Glasgow works of Gordon and Dobson are recorded, the vagueness of their biographies, like that of Walford, suggests that Scotland's and the world's understandable interest in (obsession with) the Mackintosh circle has been to the detriment of other contemporaneous designers, that there might be a larger hinterland yet to be examined in detail.

Dobson was the acknowledged Art Nouveau designer and his partnership with Gordon brief, little more than the time taken to design and construct Riselaw House. Consequently the house is rather more west coast than east in its form and details, the white harling contrasting sharply with the over-sized red sandstone hood lintel at the entrance. It is built high in a commanding situation on the spur of Buckstone Snab to the west of the Braid Hill at the edge of the Comiston Estate. The house overlooks the Braidburn Valley with panoramic views north and west to the city centre 10 kilometres distant. When first built, imbued with the confidence of a new century, and with Edinburgh's 19th-century southern expansion halted a kilometre and half away to the north, it must have been a stunning sight to those entering or leaving Edinburgh on the old road to Penicuik to the southwest.

Bungalow and villa development in the 1920s and '30s has since robbed Riselaw House of its isolation but, nonetheless, it declines to fade into a background of other rather less distinguished white-painted, red pantiled or grey-slated dwellings.

PRIVATE DWELLING

Lion Chambers

Lion Chambers

56

170–2 Hope Street, Glasgow, 1905

Architects
John Gaff Gillespie (1870–1926)
James Salmon (1873–1924) of
Salmon, Son & Gillespie

WITHIN THREE YEARS of the completion of The Hatrack and on another tight urban plot Salmon, Son and Gillespie designed Lion Chambers for the Glasgow solicitor William Black, a member of the Glasgow Arts Club, to house a shop on the ground floor, his office immediately above and artists' studios above that. The street frontage of corner tower and gable bay presents as a mix of Art Nouveau, Arts & Crafts and Baronial motives, a design, largely it is thought, from the hand of Gillespie, and development of Salmon's earlier more florid Art Nouveau style. It is the simplicity of the shallow bays of the partially visible service lane elevation which hints at what was to come later in the new century.

Lion Chambers was wholly built in reinforced concrete – the first such building in Scotland – using the Hennebique system patented in France in 1892 for which LG Mouchel of Woking, Salmon's builder, was one of two licensees in the United Kingdom.

Issues with the durability of the novel and complex Hennebique system and the thinness of the concrete external walls in the damp Glasgow climate (precipitation twice that of Paris, a challenge generally for exposed reinforced concrete construction throughout Scotland) has rendered Lion Chambers structurally unsound. It is unoccupied, covered in a protective mesh, waiting for a conservation angel to buy and restore it (Glasgow City Council recently offered it for sale for £1).

NO PUBLIC ACCESS

NEARBY: 32 ST VINCENT ST. CHURCH
50 ST VINCENT CHAMBERS
54 WILLOW TEA ROOMS
98 QUEEN STREET STATION

St Peter's RC Church

St Peter's RC Church
Falcon Avenue, Edinburgh 1906–7

Architect
Sir Robert Lorimer (1864–1929)

ST PETER'S REVEALS the extent to which architects of the early years of the 20th century had freed themselves of the heavy historicist burden of Revivalism and Eclecticism and felt confident enough in their own abilities and artistic judgement to indulge in the playful treatment of such styles or, indeed, in no style at all. Robert Lorimer said of St Peter's that it was:

> to be in the upstanding and primitive manner. All white-washed brick inside… with as much Italian flavour as is compatible with its locality and low costs.

In the blockiness of the larger masonry elements it has echoes of ES Prior's primitive Freestyle monumentalism at St Andrew's, Roker, England, 1905, while in the smaller details there is a Celtic delicacy and complexity. The particularly fine ironwork is by Lorimer's regular blacksmith and metalworker, Thomas Haden. The interior is almost Lutheran in its simplicity and the overall sense is of an economic late Arts & Crafts ethos.

The diminutive ensemble – it contains church, tower, presbytery and school hall clustered round a square court on a tight site among the high, wide and handsome Morningside sandstone tenements – has the feeling of a church at the heart of a small Italian village or that it's been shrunk to fit the site. Nonetheless, its compactness and detail is quite exquisite in its dense urban location and the little partially enclosed square with its gravel, stone flags and planting is a sudden relief from all those big tenements.

RESTRICTED ACCESS
NEARBY: 33 LAMMERBURN
34 BARCLAY BRUNTSFIELD

RW Forsyth's

RW Forsyth's

30 Princes Street, Edinburgh, 1906–7 and 1923–5

Architect
Sir John James Burnet (1857–1938)

BASED INITIALLY IN Glasgow, Burnet became not merely Scotland's premier architect of the first third of the 20th century, but also the United Kingdom's. Beaux-Arts trained, Burnet contrived, from the Renaissance Revival styles and his many American contacts, a highly distinctive and influential commercial Baroque such that it was known, and adopted by other British architects, as 'Burnetian Baroque'.

Forsyth's, for the department store magnate RW Forsyth, was the culmination of Burnet's earlier Glasgow work and of the Civil Service Association Building of 1903 (now Hollister) nearby in George Street. It was the first all-steel-framed building in Scotland and the second in the UK (by one year). It demonstrates how, throughout Britain in the early years of the new century, structural and constructional innovation was almost invariably masked by a Revival masonry skin. The building was extended in 1923 by one larger bay westwards on Princes Street and, by means of linking bridges, across Meuse Lane to St Andrew's Square.

Forsyth's closed in 1985 and the building became a Topshop fashion outlet. The upper floors were converted to hotel use in 2012 and the building fabric restored 2012–16 by 3DReid Architects and Sharkey Construction. The four-year removal and restoration of the gilded sculpture was a local cause célèbre in that it was linked to Topshop owner Philip Green's very public fall from grace in 2020. The building changed hands again in 2022 and a new hotelier, Rok, has plans for further internal upgrading.

NO PUBLIC ACCESS

NEARBY: 26 ROYAL HIGH SCHOOL
48 MANSFIELD TRAQUAIR
95 MURPHY HOUSE

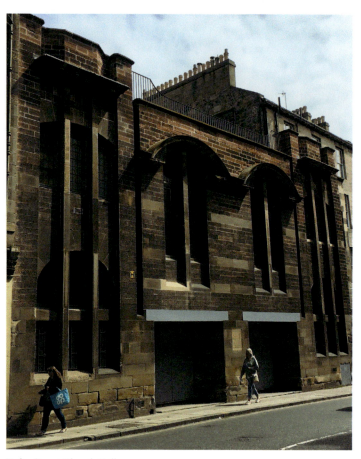

Duke Street Church Halls

Duke Street Church Halls

71–77 Duke Street, Leith, Edinburgh, 1907

Architect
James Marr Johnston (1871–1934)

THE WORK OF local architects, working in relative isolation from their more celebrated peers, consumed by that work, although not isolated from current architectural movements, contributing significantly to their communities has always appealed to me. Johnston was such an architect in Leith (up till 1928 a separate burgh) with shops, warehouses, churches, engineering works, a poorhouse and private houses to his name. In such a situation, architectural ambition is often circumscribed by client caution and budgetary constraints. Occasionally a work slips through which gives some indication of what might have been possible in more propitious circumstances.

Duke Street Church Halls presents as the rugged, rectilinear Scottish Art Nouveau more often encountered in Glasgow and the west. The mullions of the two floors of Diocletian windows of the end pavilions have been projected into continuous pilasters providing support for the projecting canopies above which interact with the canted parapets. Just below the canopies are chequerboard panels of variegated coloured sandstone. The central bay is differentiated from the pavilions by a deep groove which ends where the steel lintels, which align with the transoms in the adjacent Diocletian windows, sit over the doors. The arched windows beneath the shallow Mannerist-arched element have Gothic tracery of the kind seen at St John's, Portobello 53. This is a clever, knowledgeable and expressive design.

I passed this building every schoolday for 13 years, attended Cub Scout meetings there and, in schoolboy ignorance, gave it no mind. I cannot recall the interior.

NO PUBLIC ACCESS

Shop and flats for John Paris

John Paris Building

60

11 South Street, Bo'ness, 1907 and 1979

Architects
Matt Steele (1878–1937)
William 'Bill' Cadell (b.1933)

STEELE, UNLIKE VIRTUALLY all of his Scottish contemporaries, had little interest in traditional Scottish architecture or the Baronial. In Falkirk Council records, there is a single drawing by him dated 1909 of a traditional 'House in the Style of Old Grange' to be erected on Linlithgow Road – but no evidence of it ever having been built. Rather, Steele's influences were the work of the English Free-Style architect CFA Voysey and the European Secessionists. The arched shopfront is directly comparable to the 'Boberg' doorway found in contemporaneous Finnish Romantic architecture in Helsinki, Turku and Tampere. Certain of Steele's Bo'ness clients were importers of Finnish timber for use as pitprops.

At South Street, Steele would appear to have borrowed the entrance front of Pastures, Rutland of 1901 by Voysey right down to the tripartite windows and the projecting eaves on coved corbels. However, the little building had to wait until 1979 and local architect Bill Cadell's intervention for it to present as Steele had intended in the original drawing. John Paris had baulked at the adventurousness and possible expense of Steele's shopfront design and had had a conventional rectilinear version built instead.

Paris's provides a focal point but not obtrusively so in a street of mostly late 18th and early 19th-century tenements. Its modest distinction demonstrates a skill that many architects seemed to lose in the later decades of the 20th century.

PRIVATE DWELLING OVER SHOP
NEARBY: 63 HIPPODROME

Artist's studio

Artist's Studio

23–39 Queensferry Street, Edinburgh, 1909

Architect
William HA Ross (n.d.)
(active 1890–1910)

HERE IS A strange fragment of Glasgow Art Nouveau at the very edge of Edinburgh's Classical New Town just behind Robert Adam's Charlotte Square.

Ross designed the blue-painted attic artist's studio – there is a large north-facing window on Charlotte Lane, since painted out – in 1909. It has a perfect Glasgow Art Nouveau dormer window, right down to the gridded leaded glazing with multi-coloured glass roundels where the lead kames meet; a generously glazed leaded domed turret and finial; and the clever incorporation of the original Georgian swept gable and Diocletian window of the chimney stack into an Art Nouveau sensibility.

Was it for Ross? Unlikely, as he seems to have worked from his home addresses in Keir Street, behind the College of Art, or from Marchmont Crescent. If not for Ross, then, who was the artist? Were the Ross family, Sir William and Hugh, who were well-known Victorian painters related, although both were deceased by 1873? Could it have been designed for their progeny? William HA Ross was certainly of an age to be a grandson; a studio for a sibling or a cousin, perhaps.

Ross left little recorded trace other than a neat Arts & Crafts terrace at Greenbank Terrace, Edinburgh, from 1908, which has some fine ashlar masonry.

Sometimes, it's not the story the building tells but the one we can project on to it that matters; I could see myself living and working there.

PRIVATE DWELLING

Grangewells exterior

Grangewells stairwell

Grangewells

Acre Road, Muirhouses, Bo'ness, 1911

Architect
Matt Steele

DESPITE THE CONSTRUCTED evidence that Steele's work was influenced by Voysey and the Secessionists, this building is described by many authorities as a 'Glasgow School', even a 'Mackintosh' house. This shows the extent to which Mackintosh has left commentators with few other popularly identifiable characteristics on which to base their descriptions. At Grangewells this has been compounded by the painting out of most of the grey sandstone in a deadly black and the harling in a stark white in the late 1980s and which has given the house a comic-book Glasgow School look. The metal gate is of recent construction.

So, while I'm on this architectural revisionism let's look more closely at the significant gable. This is quite unlike any prominent gable in Mackintosh's work, two of which are illustrated here (entries 51 and 88) and which are asymmetric and dynamic. Steele's gable, by way of contrast, is symmetrical and static, focused on the projecting semi-circular bay with its hemispherical half-dome and the blank wall above, neither feature employed by Mackintosh. They, and the arrangement of glazing bars in the windows, are, however, to be found in the Helsinki work of Lars Sonck and Armas Lindgren, the Finnish National Romantic architects, especially in their later classicised designs. I've recounted above the Finnish connection. Steele, a noted sailor, may well have journeyed with his timber-importer client to the Baltic, where he could have seen Finnish work. Houses like Grangewells have their own stories and don't need to be conflated with Mackintosh's, even by association, for their justification.

PRIVATE DWELLING

Hippodrome (John Taylor extension on left)

Hippodrome from original 1912 photograph

Hippodrome

63

North Street, Bo'ness, 1911 and 1936

Architects
Matt Steele
John Taylor (1884–1942)

A WORD OF explanation: I have included a drawing taken from a contemporary photograph. Taylor's 1936 addition obscures the clarity of Steele's original design. I wrote of it in 2010:

[The Hippodrome] opened for business on 12 March 1912... Given the Lumière Brothers first presentations of 'cinématographie' took place on 28 December 1895 in a café on the Boulevard des Capucines, that the first purpose-built cinema in the world, the Electric Theatre in Los Angeles, opened in 1902, and the first in Great Britain, the Biograph, London, 1905, the Hippodrome is a remarkable act of confidence and prescience by Louis Dickson [Steele's client]. What is also remarkable is that, while early cinemas were either housed in existing theatres or, if newly constructed, adopted almost without exception the flamboyant Baroque or Rococo architecture of the theatre or music hall. Steele produced a curving volumetric design quite startling in its modernity and not surpassed in Britain until designers began to emulate the stream-lined forms of Erich Mendelsohn's seminal Universum Cinema, Berlin, 1927.

The Hippodrome is an Art Nouveau of Steele's conception unique in Scotland at the time it was built and an intimation, of the architecture of the 1930s. Had it been built in one of the larger cities it might have gained attention at the time and made a contribution to the development of modern architecture in Scotland.

It was restored by the Pollock Hammond Partnership in 2007 for Falkirk Council who continue to operate it as a cinema. It is widely known for its festival of silent movies.

CHECK WEBSITE FOR OPENING TIMES
NEARBY: 60 JOHN PARIS BUILDING

Early Modernism: 64–74

WHILE THE CUBIST and Futurist experimentation of the early 1900s and reaction to the horrors and destruction of WWI resulted in the many forms of Modernism that sprouted in continental Europe in the 1920s, Scotland, in the immediate aftermath of war, reached back to a relatively settled pre-war time and the further development of the architectural ideas prevalent then. Burnet's commercial Baroque became part of a more general Classical revival in large institutional buildings, as was also the case in Europe, while other buildings might appear in a variety of traditional Scottish garbs. Structural innovation was still concealed within largely masonry skins whether Baroque, Classical or Traditional. Art Deco cinemas, leisure facilities and shops and infrequent white-walled, flat-roofed houses constituted a limited canon of Modernism.

The arms-production boom of the war years was replaced by the slump of 1921, the interruption of the General Strike of 1926, the Wall Street Crash of 1929 and the subsequent Depression, not relieved in Scotland until the totemic completion of No. 534, subsequently named ss *Queen Mary* on Clydeside in 1936. Likewise, the Scottish city, the great generator of architectural opportunity in the 19th-century, was in stasis with 'growth' represented only by the amalgamation of smaller burghs with larger.

One looks in vain, then, for an equivalent architectural adventurousness and experimentation as is to be found in France, Germany, the Netherlands and Czechoslovakia as Scotland tempered Modernity with older models or with less extreme influences from the continent. Architecture in Scotland in the 1920s and '30s simply took a different road.

Scottish National War Memorial, entrance

Scottish National War Memorial, Shrine

Scottish National War Memorial
Crown Square, Edinburgh Castle, 1924–7

64

Architect
Sir Robert Lorimer

WHAT ARCHITECTURAL OPPORTUNITY there was in plenty in the 1920s was the design and construction of military cemeteries and war memorials throughout the Great War battlefields and in every village, burgh and city at home. Robert Lorimer designed approximately 40 military cemeteries and war memorials at home and abroad in that first post-war decade.

For someone of my 1940s generation, The War Memorial was a place of occasional silent pilgrimage, taken by parents whose war experience was recent and raw, to look at the pages of the book of the war dead wherein was inscribed the name of an uncle I never knew. The curiosity of the exposed basalt at the highest point of Castle Rock as it burst through the floor of the Shrine of Lorimer's imagining to support the altar was of rather greater interest to a five-year-old. The Gallery of Honour which fronts it is, with true Scottish economy, a conversion of an old barracks; Lorimer, commissioned in 1919, had a rather grander proposal to begin with which met with considerable opposition. Visiting the building many years later, I was struck by the way in which the combination of strength and delicacy of Lorimer's compromise design respected and commemorated the dead while eschewing the bombast of martial triumph. The acknowledged 'primitivism' of St Peter's RC Church 57 has acquired a specifically Scottish flavour. Be warned, like the Wallace Monument, this is a stiff climb; there are no lifts.

CHECK WEBSITE FOR OPENING TIMES
NEARBY: 20 GLADSTONE'S LAND
38 NATIONAL MUSEUM
45 CENTRAL LIBRARY
89 MUSEUM OF SCOTLAND

Reid Memorial Church

Reid Memorial Church

Blackford Avenue, Edinburgh, 1929–33

Architect
Leslie Grahame Thomson (1896–1974)

DISRUPTION OF THE Church of Scotland in the 19th century resulted in several new denominations, the Free Church of Scotland being one, becoming the United Free Church in 1919 through subsequent amalgamation. The Reid Memorial was initiated as a United Free Church to be constructed, on another site, from the estate of the last of the eponymous William Reid's childless sons who died in 1921. By the time work began the United Free Church and the Church of Scotland had reunited. It has been alleged that Thomson stole this commission from Lorimer whose assistant he had been until he set up in independent practice in 1927.

In content – church, session house, vestries, hall and cloister – the Reid has, on a generous site, what Lorimer was required to shoehorn in at St Peter's (see entry 57). The dramatic site planning of the Reid Memorial represents an arresting example of late monumental Arts & Crafts architecture, possibly even its Scottish apotheosis. But what a grand way to bring an architectural chapter to a close. The recessed west window above arched entrance porch commands the gushet site at the busy junction of five roads. Viewed orthogonally along Charterhall Road and obliquely from Blackford Avenue the tall nave, transepts and tower give no hint of the modest domesticity of the stone-flagged meditative cloister sheltering, almost mediaevally, beneath the tower at the east end. The details are lifted successfully, from the Lorimer playbook, the primitivism of St Peter's and the War Memorial evident in the treatment of the wallheads.

RESTRICTED ACCESS
NEARBY: 67 LANE HOUSE
79 SILLITTO HOUSE

St Andrew's House, south elevation

St Andrew's House, north elevation

St Andrew's House

Regent Road, Edinburgh, 1933–9

Architect
Thomas Tait (1882–1954) of Burnet, Tait & Lorne

ST ANDREW'S HOUSE rises out of the igneous crag, seeming to be part of it, a significant 20th-century addition to Edinburgh's Acropolis, the Calton Hill.

The convoluted history of this building and what it represented in terms of Scottish autonomy began in 1912. It was intended to house civil servants engaged in the administration, not legislation, of government functions in Scotland. Despite this admirable devolving intent, such was London's habitual controlling inclination that, with the matter still undecided 20 years later, John Buchan MP (Lord Tweedsmuir) author of *The Thirty-Nine Steps,* speaking in the House of Commons debate of November 1932, demanded:

an outward and visible sign of Scottish nationhood… [for] we are in danger very soon of reaching the point where Scotland will have nothing distinctive to show the world.

Tait's appointment the following year was the perfect answer to Buchan's plea. Motives from Frank Lloyd Wright and Willem Marinus Dudok are married to an Edinburgh tradition of building in stone on hills. The sculptural terms on the entry front represent Statecraft, Health, Agriculture, Fisheries, Education and Architecture, all of which were administrative activities at St Andrew's House in 1939, finally in 1997 became the legislative responsibilities at the Scottish parliament at Holyrood. St Andrew's House currently accommodates part of the Scottish civil service.

NO PUBLIC ACCESS

NEARBY: **26** ROYAL HIGH SCHOOL
58 RW FORSYTH'S
95 MURPHY HOUSE

The Lane House from garden

Broughton Place, Broughton

The Lane House

46a Dick Place, Grange, Edinburgh, 1934

Architect
William Kininmonth (1908–88)

TOM NORMAND'S VIEW of Scotland and Modernism in the 1930s was that there was

> a kind of conservatism to this modernism, for it consistently remained within the boundaries of established taste... the very foundation of radical avant-garde activity was absent. This absence was shaped by a temperamental disinclination for Scottish artists to engage in theory...

The Lane House, built by Kininmonth for himself, is one of the few convincing Scottish examples of that more European Modernism. I visited the house in 1994 when it was occupied by Kininmonth's son-in-law – Kininmonth lived in it till his death in 1988. It is built on part of the former garden ground of Frederick Pilkington's Grange Park House (1856–70). What stood out was the sweeping view south to Blackford Hill and the easy interaction of modernity and homeliness; the sense that one gets from some of the smaller Arts & Crafts or Art Nouveau houses such as Windyhill, Kilmacolm, 1901, by Mackintosh. It even boasts a 'free' ground floor plan.

When originally built, the flush-pointed perpends and deep-grooved beds of the exposed brickwork were lime-washed which, together with the concrete copes, sills and surrounds to windows and doors, gave the house a much more horizontal Dutch or German Expressionist aspect than its present white harling, added to improve weathering. One can imagine the sensation it created in the douce Grange when first revealed.

PRIVATE DWELLING

NEARBY: 65 REID MEMORIAL CHURCH
79 SILLITTO HOUSE

Dunfermline Fire Station

Dunfermline Fire Station

Carnegie Drive, Dunfermline, 1934

Architect
James Shearer (1881–1962)

SHEARER WAS ONE of Burnet's senior assistants and like many of his generation greatly influenced by him and by Lorimer. His work was traditional in appearance although structurally adventurous. The reading room of his traditionalist Dunfermline Library extension of 1913 was spanned by the largest reinforced concrete vault of the time at 35ft (10.7m). Nevertheless, there was no other obvious precedent in Shearer's work for the Fire Station.

There are three explanations given for his shift in architectural style. The first is that his younger brother Thomas Smith Shearer had recently returned from practice in London bringing with him the latest design ideas. However, James Ernest Franck, for whom Tom Shearer worked, was no ground-breaker. The second, given by Shearer's colleague, William Dey, was that he 'was making an explicit attempt to introduce Scottish feeling into the modern movement'. The third, told me by Shearer's assistant Marcus Johnston, was that the Town Council insisted on a flat roof with a tall parapet to conceal the chimney stacks and maintain the Modern appearance.

There is considerable evidence of the influence of Dudok's Hilversum work in the design of the fire station that imputes a more determined effort on the part of Shearer to update his architectural thinking than as the consequence of three apocryphal stories. Shearer visited Dudok in 1952 in order to invite him to Scotland to address Scottish architects which suggests some sort of a connection between the two architects.

NO PUBLIC ACCESS

One of the blocks of Jenners flats

Jenners Flats

1–48 Ravelston Garden, Edinburgh 1935–6

69

Architects
Andrew Neil (1899–1972) and
Robert Hurd (1905–63)

THIS ELEGANT GROUP of three blocks of 'butterfly' planned flats and garages – known for their letting agents – is rare in Scotland. It is generally thought that Neil was the designer; he had travelled widely in France and Italy in 1926, his first wife was German and he followed developments in German architecture closely. Hurd was emphatically the traditionalist although he claimed of the design that he was 'aiming for the essential character of 17th-century Scots Architecture stripped of its details'.

It would seem, however, that much of that character resides in the very details that were removed.

The plan is ingenious with garage courts leading to service stairs and kitchen entrances concealed within the 'wings' running north and south which give on to a service zone within the flat comprising hall, kitchen and servant's bedroom. The main entrance opens off the main stair and lift, and connects to the living room and dining room, linked through large sliding doors, and with a large balcony. The main bedrooms face east or west. There is a clever device for cleanly supplying coal to an open coal fire in the living room from the service zone.

My friend the late émigré Czech urban planner Berty Hornung and I spent many a happy hour over a bottle of Moravian white in the servant's room, converted into a study, in his flat in one of these blocks, planning the exhibition of Prague Art and Architecture, held at the City Art Centre 1994.

PRIVATE DWELLING

Kirkcaldy Town House

Detail of clock tower

Kirkcaldy Town House

Wemyssfield, Kirkcaldy, 1937–53

70

> **Architects**
> David Carr (1905–86) and
> William Frederick Howard (1906–72)

FOLLOWING THE 1832 Reform Act, further legislation throughout the 19th century granted increased powers and status, including the building of town halls, to those local authorities that met certain population numbers. Into the 20th century many of those earlier town halls were showing their age while increased local authority responsibilities and growing urbanisation swelled the populations of smaller communities to a point where the building of a new town hall was a necessity resulting in a spate of architectural competitions for town halls throughout the late 1920s and 1930s.

Carr and Howard, first separately, then jointly, were inveterate competition entrants winning Kirkcaldy in 1937 with an elegant asymmetric stone-clad design. Kirkcaldy has much in common with other town halls of the period with its flat-roofed classicised Modernism such as those at the London boroughs of Walthamstow (now Waltham Forest), Hornsey, or Brent. Although town hall design was not a closed shop, in the 1930s there was something of a 'revolving door' with successful entrants becoming adjudicators of subsequent competitions. This might explain how a limited number of architectural motives were in constant circulation in these designs throughout the period.

WWII halted construction and the partnership stuttered on into the late 1940s when Howard left for Canada. Kirkcaldy Town House was completed in 1953, its design already obsolete compared to the new utilitarian architecture of the youthful Welfare State.

RESTRICTED ACCESS

Rothesay Pavilion

Rothesay Pavilion in context

Rothesay Pavilion

Argyle Street, Rothesay, 1938

71

Architects
James Carrick (1880–1940) and
James Andrew Carrick (1911–89)

FOR THE FIRST two-thirds of the 20th century, certainly before advent of cheaper air fares and package holidays to Spain in the 1960s, Glaswegians took their two weeks of the Glasgow Fair holiday in the many resort towns and islands of the Firth of Clyde such as Helensburgh, Gourock, Largs, Millport on Great Cumbrae, Dunoon, Wemyss Bay or Rothesay on the Isle of Bute. This was known as going 'doon the watter' and was serviced by numerous steam boats like the PS *Waverley*, still in operation today on inshore and coastal waters around the British Isles.

Dance halls, ice cream parlours, bandstands, parks, boating ponds and pavilions sprang up throughout the 1920s and '30s to cater for visitors. Rothesay Pavilion, won in a 1936 architectural competition by the Carrick father and son architects, contains bars, ballroom and function spaces. It is a highly effective stylistic amalgam of the two contemporary Scottish preferences in modern design: the German Expressionism of Serge Chermayeff and Erich Mendelsohn as at their De La Warr Pavilion, Bexhill-on-Sea, 1935, and the volumetric composition of Willem Marinus Dudok at Hilversum Town Hall, Netherlands, 1931.

Restoration of the Pavilion by Elder & Cannon Architects is due to complete in 2026.

CHECK WEBSITE FOR OPENING TIMES

Palace of Art

Glazing detail

Palace of Art

Bellahouston Park, Glasgow, 1938

Architects
Launcelot Hugh Ross (1885–1956)
and Thomas Tait

SOMETIMES A BUILDING is significant for what is missing as much as for what is there.

Firstly, because its context has gone. In the case of the Palace of Art that context was the avenues, terraces, cascades, pavilions, fountains and tower of the 1938 Glasgow Empire Exhibition. The Palace sat at the east end of the Scottish Avenue and was flanked by the two Scottish pavilions of which all that remains is a wide lawn.

Secondly, it's the building itself which in its studied coolness might seem to give us little to interact with. However, look again. The central range, which fronts a quadrangle, is bookended by projecting pavilions. This is close to the plan form of the Egyptian temple such as that at Edfu while that central element with its square pillars has the sense of being a pylon, an Egyptian gate. The thin slot separating the end column from the wall is a subtle device used by Alexander Thomson q.v. which gives prominence to the colonnade. The well-proportioned recently renewed (?) glazing echoes that of Le Corbusier. The rationality of the elevation is emphasised in its being constructed from approximately 60x60 cm polished concrete panels.

The tall, perfectly chosen, sans serif lettering is of a thickness to match the glazing bars below. The curved masonry planters and the contemporary handrails are an almost incidental counterpoint to the regularity of the façade. This is a perfectly conceived and modest example of a Scottish interpretation of canonic European Modernism. It deserves to be better known.

CHECK WEBSITE FOR OPENING TIMES
NEARBY: 88 HOUSE FOR AN ART LOVER

St Peter-in-Chains RC Church

St Peter-in-Chains RC Church

South Crescent Road, Ardrossan, 1938

Architects
Jack Coia (1898–1981)
of Gillespie, Kidd & Coia

MY ATTENTION HAS always focused on the completely blank southwest front of gable and tower of this church. Coia has treated them almost as one element, the gable projected little more than a brick's length beyond the tower, which sits in front of a plainer nave and choir, a device he used often. The gable presents an exaggerated Italian pointed arch, the carved stone keystone, the brick 'seam' above, the shallow pitch and tiny masonry skewputts with similar motives on the tower which seem to be entirely within the tradition of the Amsterdam School of the 1910s and '20s. Coia's St Patrick's RC Church, Orangefield, Greenock, 1934–5, is generically similar and both have much in common with the Expressionist Church of the Holy Martyrs of Gorkum, 1928, at Linnaeushof, Amsterdam by Alexander Kropholler. As we have seen, Netherlands architectural influence was a frequent constituent of Scottish Modernism in the 1930s.

There is the sense that this church, like other examples from the 1930s, is an end not a beginning. Johnny Rodger wrote this about Jack Coia's practice; it could stand for all Scottish architecture on the eve of WWII:

> But if [the] achievement of [1956 to 1987] arose from the launching pad of the reputation established by the practice before the 1939–45 war then any real comparison of those two bodies of work separated in time reveals them to be something very different in terms of historical, technological, architectonic and programmatic aims and influences.

RESTRICTED ACCESS

Italian Chapel

Italian Chapel interior

Italian Chapel

Lambholm, Orkney, 1942–4

Artisans
Domenico Chiocchetti, Guiseppe Palumbi, Giovanni Pennisi and others

SCOTLAND HAS A long tradition of welcoming immigrant families who chose to abandon the Italian sun for our cooler climes to make a profound and positive impact on Scottish culture and character. Chiocchetti and his colleagues, as WWII prisoners-of-war, did not choose to come to Lambholm but, in being required to, made their own unique contribution to Scotland. The tiny island of Lambholm – you can walk round it in less than three-quarters of an hour – was home to Camp 60, an airfield, a harbour and the manufacturing plant that made the concrete blocks for the Churchill Barriers which secured Scapa Flow and the North Atlantic fleet from submarine attack. From scrap material salvaged from the plant the Italian POWs fabricated a memory of home and a place to worship within a pair of corrugated iron Nissan huts. Chiocchetti returned in 1960 and in 1964 to initiate restoration which has been an ongoing project ever since. Many of the Italians, although not Chiocchetti, returned in 1992 for the 50th anniversary of the Chapel and a celebratory Mass.

I first encountered the chapel in 1971 when on a family holiday housed in a caravan on what is now the Chapel car park. In those days, there was but a trickle of visitors and we were not disturbed.

CHECK WEBSITE FOR OPENING TIMES

Late Modernism: 75–88

MODERNISM'S ARRIVAL IN Scotland was delayed. The precepts of the European leading lights of the 1920s and '30s only now, post-WWII, began to appear in built form in any quantity in Scotland due in part to the limited pre-war opportunities to build and partly to an innate conservatism. This resulted in nearly three decades of Modernist experimentation in the originating countries, not Scotland, having opened up a wide range of stylistic possibilities which were simultaneously available or which cycled with increasing rapidity, almost as if a missing or misplaced part of Scottish architectural history were being fabricated, in all senses of the word, all at once.

This was facilitated, at least until 1975, through the wholesale and near-consensual adoption of Modernism by the agencies of the Welfare State, commerce and industry as their architectural model whether in the provision of housing, healthcare, leisure facilities, schools, offices, factories, etc. Long-overdue slum clearance, inner-city regeneration, and bomb damage restitution was married to the theoretical models of the 1930s and an architectural ambition frustrated by the lack of opportunity in the previous un-Modern decades. Great works were produced but the failures were so egregious that they have tended to monopolise commentary. Suffice to say that novelty was too often misinterpreted as innovation.

As the century progressed architects in Scotland journeyed from a late 1930s Expressionism, to the ethos of Le Corbusier, to the Californian Case Study houses, to Brutalism, to Vernacularism, to the 'Nordic cool' of the Cambridge School, to industrial Process to Post-Modernism while reinterpreting these styles for a Scottish environment and culture.

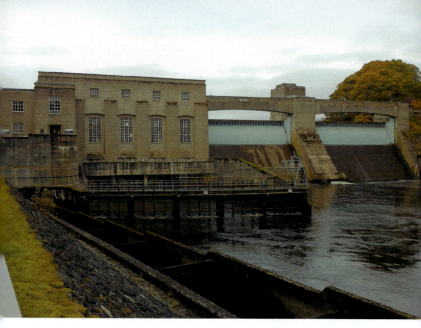

Pitlochry dam, generating station and fish ladder

Pitlochry Dam

River Tummel, Pitlochry 1947–51

Architect
Harold Tarbolton (1869–1947)
Engineers
Sir Alexander Gibb & Co

IN 1988 PETER PAYNE wrote that

> [m]any of those who tramp the hills of Scotland, often in the mists and rain, surely entertain the thought that there must be further scope for harnessing the free-falling, turbulent Highland waters for the production of energy.

This was not an especially novel observation as the Highland Water Power Bill was considered in Parliament in 1899 followed by the Loch Ericht Water and Electricity Power Act in 1912 with approval for the scheme granted in 1922. World wars, the Depression and substantial opposition delayed matters until the 1940s when the dynamic Secretary of State for Scotland Tom Johnson conjoined the creation of hydro-electric power with the revival of the Highland stone industry and community projects. The Loch Ericht scheme was but one of many which were of significance in the Highland economy.

The River Tummel was dammed at Pitlochry to form Loch Faskally which was but the end point of a complex network of feeder lochs and rivers that provided the motive power for the generating station. Construction works were undertaken by Sir Alexander Gibb's company who employed German and Italian POWs and the thrillingly named Donegal Tunnelling Tigers, a team of widely-travelled Irish tunnelling experts. Tarbolton, who had designed his first electrical project in 1902 was engaged to bring some contemporary architectural merit to the dam and generating station although he would not see it through to completion.

CHECK WEBSITE FOR OPENING TIMES

Telephone Exchange, expressionist window

Telephone Exchange

116 Fountainbridge, Edinburgh 1948–52

Architect
Stewart Sim (1898–1988)
HM Ministry of Works

THIS IS ONE of a few buildings that stylistically span the historic divide of WWII which suggests to me it may have been conceived prior to 1939. In its conception it is wholly Expressionistic in the manner of the German architect Erich Mendelsohn who, on his escape from Nazi Germany in 1936, spent some brief time at Edinburgh College of Art. The rectilinear block to the left houses the highly visible exchange equipment while the lower round-ended block to the right of office and staff accommodation. Tying these disparate elements together is the genius of the vertical stair tower; its tall window is allowed to slip expressively over the top of the curved block without apparent corner support. Modern Movement orthodoxy would have had the Exchange white cement-rendered but this being Edinburgh it is clad in sandstone ashlar.

Until very recently the Exchange, with exception of the splendid St Cuthbert's Cooperative Society offices and bakery across the street, was surrounded by low-grade, one and two-storey building. New construction close-by has provided the Exchange with an elevated setting and has itself influenced some adjacent works. The advent of the mobile phone, tending to reduce the need for the Exchange has contributed a panoply of rooftop aerials in a manner the Russian Constructivists would have approved of. This is a building that had to wait 60 years to come into its own.

NO PUBLIC ACCESS

NEARBY: 37 FOUNTAINBRIDGE TENEMENT

St Paul's RC Church

St Paul's interior

St Paul's RC Church
Warout Road, Glenrothes, 1956–8

Architects
Isi Metzstein (1928–2012) and
Andy MacMillan (1928–2014) of
Gillespie, Kidd & Coia

THIS EXQUISITE LITTLE church constructed in Glenrothes, Scotland's second post-war new town, represents a sea-change in Scottish architecture. The lack of opportunity of the 1920s and '30s was replaced by post-war reconstruction and Metzstein and MacMillan, graduates of the Mackintosh School of Architecture at Glasgow School of Art, were among the first architects whose training post-dates 1945. The lessons of the Modern Movement, in particular those of Le Corbusier, were not only learned but were incorporated into a Scottish idiom.

This is a building about backs and fronts, It splays out from the glazed entrance screen to meet the blank façade of the east wall and tower which has its own glazed screen. In the use of the thick and thin irregularly spaced glazing bars as the principal decorative element, in the contrast of solid and void and in the paratactically located window on the priest's accommodation St Paul's embodies abstractly some of what MacMillan had learned from his abiding passion for the work of Charles Rennie Mackintosh. The glazed screens also reveal MacMillan and Metzstein's concern with bringing natural light to the altar at the heart of the church. The manipulation and directed use of natural light was to feature in all their subsequent church designs. At St Paul's a tight budget has been transcended by an inventive economy of means which will be the touchstone of much of the best of the coming architecture.

RESTRICTED ACCESS

Canongate Housing

Canongate Housing

78

65–71, 97–103 Canongate, 1–3 Brown's Close
Edinburgh, 1961–9

Architect
Sir Basil Spence, Glover and Ferguson

THE CANONGATE UNDERWENT substantial restoration and new build in the early 1950s, mostly stylistically faithful to the earlier building stock, some obsequiously others awkwardly so, some exhibiting a frivolous 'Festival of Britain' aesthetic. By far the best is Chessel's Court.

Spence and colleagues took a different approach. Focusing on Reid Court and Canongate Manse and with Reid house itself to be adjoined (on the left of the image) they set up their two blocks of one and two bedroom flats with shops and bar on the ground floor to frame and integrate the court into the Canongate. They took cues from the existing buildings – masonry construction, vertically oriented windows, prominent architraves to windows and doors, external stairs and balcony access (to the rear), coloured harled walling – and combined them with elements from their recent practice at Sussex University – *béton brut* arches, piloti, balconies – substituting stone for brick, all under monopitch roofs at right angles to the street. This muscular ensemble is quite masterful and absolutely of its time – the 1960s – yet it respects and includes and adds to its 17th-century setting proving that there's more than one way to 'fit in'.

In 2022, this block underwent extensive fabric, heating and ventilation upgrading which revealed the substantial technical and capital cost challenges in 'retrofitting' mid-century construction in listed buildings to improve performance in use, reduce running costs and carbon emissions.

PRIVATE DWELLING

NEARBY: **91** SCOTTISH PARLIAMENT

Sillitto House

Sillitto House

32 Charterhall Road, Edinburgh, 1962

Architects
James Morris (1931–2006) and
Robert Steedman (b.1929)

I'VE SELECTED THE Sillitto House rather than Morris and Steedman's Avisfield, Cramond, 1952–5, which is featured in most architectural texts but is only fleetingly visible from the top deck of a number 41 bus speeding citywards.

While foreign travel was significant to architects throughout the 20th century it is sometimes difficult to ascertain from cryptic travel accounts either what they had been looking at or to what extent they had incorporated that seen in their own work. Not so with both Morris and Steedman who were widely travelled in Europe and the United States gaining experience with Louis Kahn, Philip Johnson, Alfred Roth (Marcel Breuer's associate) and the influential landscape architect Ian McHarg all of which placed them in the heart of international Modernism at this time. Moreover, Steedman spent some time in Kyoto, Japan.

These influences were to be subsumed and transformed in their joint practice. They are clearly visible in this house with its panoramic view north over central Edinburgh from its dramatic setting on the flank of Blackford Hill. There are echoes of Frank Lloyd Wright's Sturges House, Brentwood, California, or of the California Case Study houses of the 1940s and '50s while, with its defensive lower floor and elaborated upper floor it allows reflections on the Scottish tower house. The Sillitto House is confidently Modern and confidently Scottish at one and the same time.

PRIVATE DWELLING

NEARBY: 65 REID MEMORIAL CHURCH

Gala Fairydean stadium

Gala Fairydean, minimal structure

Gala Fairydean Stadium
Nether road, Galashiels, 1963–5

Architect
Peter Womersley (1923–93)
Engineer Ove Arup

IN AN ALL-TOO-BRIEF Scottish sojourn between 1955 and 1977, émigré Yorkshireman Peter Womersley left a profound and distinctive Modernist mark on Scottish architecture, especially in the Borders, spanning the delicacy of his domestic work such as High Sunderland, near Galashiels, and the Brutalism – for want of a better descriptor – of his larger-scale public work such as the Nuffield Transplant Unit at the Western General Hospital, Edinburgh.

From the inverted concrete pyramids of the turnstile roofs to the triangular extrusions of stand and canopy, seemingly barely connected together by four thin concrete fins separated by frameless glazing, this little stand has a confidence and energy appropriate to 'the beautiful game' lacking in many an international stadium. Womersley's ingenious design was brought to a 'look-no-hands' practical realisation by engineering pioneers Ove Arup fresh from making Jörn Utzon's problematic sketches of interconnecting shells buildable at the altogether grander Sydney Opera House, 1957–73.

The transience of commerce has meant that, with a few exceptions, the Borders textile industry which, in its time, could engender a construction as significant this in a sma burgh, would itself largely go elsewhere and the building over time lost some of its shine. Architects Reiach & Hall and structural engineers David Narro Associates completed an expert and sensitive restoration of the stand in 2022.

BOOKING REQUIRED

Andrew Melville Hall

Andrew Melville Hall, detail of rooms and corridor

Andrew Melville Hall

St Andrew's University, North Haugh, St Andrews
1963–8

Architect
James Stirling (1926–1992)

THIS BUILDING PERHAPS demonstrates most clearly the core ideas of what is known as Brutalism or sometimes New Brutalism. There is no 'Old' Brutalism. The 'brutal' part derives from the French *béton brut* which means 'raw concrete' and describes the manner of its use as universal material in such buildings where rough and smooth finishes are contrasted much as is random rubble and ashlar work in masonry construction.

Significant Brutalist design tactics are dramatic planning. In the case of North Haugh in site planning, the splayed plan permits sunlight into the court and its orientation with its back to the southwest responds to the wise instructions of the builders on Lewis. In building planning, the long section of the building is designed to follow the fall in the land; in the plan the student rooms are formed and clearly expressed as discrete cellular or modular units where the windows are angled to afford views northeast to the North Sea; circulation is defined and represented by the glazed corridors; and the expressive emphasis on the verticality and horizontality of structure and service ducts is used as framing or containing devices.

Andrew Melville Hall is a series of firsts: the first, and only, design by James Stirling in his native Scotland; his first solo design since his split from James Gowan; his first use of a prefabricated panel system, not without its faults; and the first, and only, element in a larger scheme of three such buildings on this site. Restoration work is being undertaken over the four summers of 2023–6.

NO PUBLIC ACCESS

Above and below: Cumbernauld Town Centre

Cumbernauld Town Centre

Cumbernauld, 1963–7

82

Architects
Leslie Hugh Wilson (1913–85),
Geoffrey Copcutt (1928–97) and
others of Cumbernauld Development
Corporation

NO BUILDING IN Scotland divides public and professional opinion quite like Cumbernauld Town Centre. Cumbernauld was designated Scotland's third new town in 1955 and conceived as an integrated town centre of one continuous and continuously extendable structure – a megastructure – sited over the principal road, surrounded by residential areas that accessed it by pedestrian paths. The megastructure was a concept that had sprung up in Japan in the early 1960s with the Metabolist Group. It was entirely new and experimental. I visited it in 1967 as a student, the year it was completed. It seemed daring, relevant and prophetic, everything we were taught about Modernism in our lecture courses although some also argued that it was naïve, crude, and overconfident, a view that has grown in strength over the years. It was crisp and clean when I saw it before the materials of which it was made suffered over the succeeding 60 years of the Scottish climate and development corporation and local authority (since 1994) maintenance schedules, losing its sparkle and becoming merely old rather than the more appealing *aged*.

Cumbernauld Town Centre was certainly all the rage at the time and was awarded the RS Reynolds Memorial Award for Community Architecture by the American Institute of Architects in 1967.

See it soon. It may not be around for very much longer. Public and political dislike are likely to see its demolition and substitution by something safer, blander, easier to maintain and which won't generate any discussion about architecture.

ACCESS DURING SHOPPING HOURS

Above: Edenside
Below: Edenside level plan

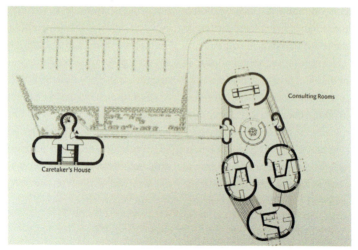

Edenside Medical Practice
Inch Road, Kelso, 1968

Architect
Peter Womersley

BUILDINGS HAVE A life. Sometimes they come to an abrupt and premature end. Sometimes they waste away because the purpose, will or finance to save them is lacking. And sometimes they are overtaken by events. Even at the date of this image – the early 1990s – changes had been made to Womersley's original design.

Today, these beautiful towers are incorporated in an enlarged health centre, subsequently constructed, which, to the credit of its designers, has made some effort to respect what was there before. However, what made the building initially so special and unique, its very specificity, is what rendered it well-nigh impossible to be extended.

Edenside was designed on a generous site to provide surgery spaces for five doctors, two couples and a singleton, round a reception and waiting area and a separate caretaker's house. The plan is of geometric clarity such as might have originated in the work of the American Louis Kahn. Three-dimensionally it reads as a Neolithic village reimagined by Le Corbusier and Charles Rennie Mackintosh with its white harling, chunky black-stained timber and blue-purple Scotch slates.

So why have I directed you to go and see it if it's a compromised design? Edenside, in its pristine form, represened a time when architects in Scotland, consciously or unconsciously, attempted to find a means of expression that married their engagement with International Modernism to their situation within an ancient tradition of building. Spence's Canongate Housing is a big toon response, Womersley's is that of the sma burgh. That context still resonates strongly at Edenside.

RESTRICTED ACCESS

Above: The Burrell Collection

The Burrell Collection interior

Burrell Collection

Pollok Park, Glasgow, 1971–84

84

Architects
Barry Gasson (b. 1935), Brit Andreson (n.d.) and John Meunier (n.d.)

FROM THE PURELY architectural historical point of view, this is another building where time moved on and left it stranded, not as Edenside in the midst of other construction, but in the course of architectural history.

It was won in competition in 1971, designed to meet the specifics of the Burrell bequest and as a more sympathetic response to the strictures of International Modernism. The 'Cambridge School, Nordic cool' exterior concealing the warmth of the interior might have been a throwback to the form of those secretive curtain-walled 13th-century castles concealing richly-modelled inner baileys significant to the Scottish psyche. However, by 1983, on completion, the subtle silence of its seemingly undemonstrative even mute exterior had been drowned out by the loudly trumpeted meanings of Post-Modernism and it had little or no impact subsequently as an architectural model for architects in Scotland. The early departure of Andreson and Meunier left the Burrell as largely Gasson's creation while his lengthy involvement in the project seems to have denied him other architectural opportunity.

The legacy of the Burrell Collection is in its public use, in the access it provides to the display of Sir William Burrell's eclectic collection, in its Nordic engagement with the landscape of Pollok Country Park by means of the great northwest window and in its sophisticated use of materials – red sandstone, polished reinforced concrete and plaster, timber structure and aluminium glazing-bars. The building was completely restored by John McAslan and Partners and the Collection redisplayed in 2016–22.

CHECK WEBSITE FOR OPENING TIMES

Eden Court Theatre

Eden Court Theatre detail

Eden Court Theatre

Waterfoot, Inverness, 1973–6 and 2007

Architects
Law & Dunbar Naismith and Page \ Park

SINCE BOTH THE Theatre Royal was destroyed in a fire in 1931 and the Empire Theatre closed in 1974 after desultory use, Inverness and the Highlands had been without modern theatre space until the Eden Court opened in 1976.

At Inverness the theatre complex comprises three parts: the original Eden Court house to the right; the theatre itself; and the 2007 extension by Page \ Park (to the left in the top image). The setting, in parkland on the west bank of the River Ness, perfectly frames the 1976 building which is planned on a hexagonal grid. In the latter part of the 20th century, angled geometry whether regular or irregular polygons became a popular planning device and means of relieving the potential sterility of the rectilinear 'box'. Although it did not come without its own challenges of occasional inconvenient spaces. Contemporaneous examples include Scottish Widows, 1967, and Mortonhall Crematorium, 1967, by Sir Basil Spence, Glover & Ferguson and the National Library of Scotland, Causewayside, 1987, by Andrew Merrilees, all Edinburgh. At Inverness a horseshoe-shaped auditorium which rises, steel-clad, above the complex is clasped by six fully glazed, slate-roofed two-tiered hexagonal elements which contain entry foyer, restaurant, bar, suspended stairs, upper foyers and milling space on several levels with views out over the River Ness. Service towers are clad in flint-aggregate blocks. It rises like a sparkling basaltic intrusion from its green surrounds. Page \ Park's extension is altogether more expressive, Constructivist, even.

CHECK WEBSITE FOR OPENING TIMES

Dundee Repertory Theatre

Dundee Repertory Theatre

86

Tay Square, Dundee, 1982

Architect
Nicoll Russell Studio

SOMETIMES A BUILDING has an impact far beyond its immediate purpose. The Dundee Repertory Company was founded in 1939 although there was a history of theatres in Dundee mostly converted to cinema use by this time. It was housed successfully if inconveniently first in the former premises of the Ancient Order of Foresters which was destroyed by fire in 1963 and then in the Dudhope Church. The present facility, both a producing and invitation theatre, was commissioned from local architects the Nicoll Russell Studios during the Recession of the late 1970s.

Once completed it had a galvanising effect on the performing and gallery arts cultures in Dundee becoming the pivot in the West End of what later became known as Dundee's 'Cultural Quarter'. This has had consequence in the inclusion of several Dundee entries in this list and is indicative of how the arts in Dundee in particular and Scotland in general have in part compensated for the loss of many traditional industries that came to an end or were ended in the late 20th century. The Rep is also the home of Scottish Dance Theatre.

Nicoll Russell's design is possibly one of the most welcoming concrete boxes one is ever likely to encounter, opening and inflecting, its great inverted glazed entry revealing the energies of front-of-house and hinting at what is to come. Such has been its success there are, as yet tentative, proposals for a new larger Rep on a nearby site.

CHECK WEBSITE FOR OPENING TIMES
NEARBY: 39 THE McMANUS GALLERY
90 DCA
97 V&A DUNDEE

21st-Century Tenement

21st-Century Tenement
Craigen Court, Stratford Street, Maryhill, Glasgow
1984–9

Architects
McGurn, Logan, Duncan & Opfer
with Ken McRae

THIS BUILDING, WON in architectural competition, came at the meeting point of several strands in Glasgow's social and architectural history. Following the emergency restoration of 5,000 damaged tenements in the aftermath of the Great Glasgow Storm of 1968, there had been a steady reappraisal of the Glasgow tenement as ideal urban dwelling form in density, practicality and in social cohesion.

At the same time, there was growing interest in the works of Alexander Thomson with several popular books on the architect published between 1979 and 1991. Architectural philosophy itself had been under Post-Modern revision since the early 1980s when Andy MacMillan was appointed Professor at the Mackintosh School of Architecture and brought with him his partner from Gillespie, Kidd & Coia, Isi Metzstein and a group of talented young practising architects as tutors of whom Peter McGurn was one.

Craigen Court is unusual in that it has six stories to the rear and only four to the front, a complex and costly arrangement, although it produced very interesting and usable floor plans and provided significant living rooms with high ceilings comparable to the Victorian tenement in the immediate vicinity. In the elevation, the designers have combined a version of Mackintosh's stair towers at the Scotland Street School with the first floor windows of Thomson's Moray Place.

PRIVATE DWELLING
NEARBY: 36 KIBBLE PALACE

House for an Art Lover north elevation

House for an Art Lover south elevation

House for an Art Lover
Bellahouston Park, Glasgow, 1988

Architects
Graham Roxburgh and Andy MacMillan, based on designs from Charles Rennie Mackintosh and Margaret MacDonald Mackintosh

CIVIL ENGINEER GRAHAM Roxburgh who had faithfully restored Craigie Hall in the 1980s, was so taken with the earlier Mackintosh interventions he encountered there that he decided he would construct the Mackintoshes' 1901 unbuilt entry for the *Haus Eines Kunstsfreundes* competition.

The competition drawings had inconsistencies and omissions and Professor Andy MacMillan was engaged to bring order to the portfolio and this is the origin of the controversy that surrounds this building. Of necessity, where the originals were lacking, MacMillan's new drawings were interpretations of what might have been designed. This inexactitude was compounded in that it was known Mackintosh changed details on site so even what seemed fixed in the original drawings might not have been so in realisation.

There is an art-historical objection that awards inviolable status as work of art to the architect's original design which, arguably for the reasons given above, is represented in the drawings but not in the building. It is not clear quite why this occurs when, say, a conductor's interpretation of a score is deemed a valid artwork, given that the score requires many others to bring the work to fruition.

Let's just enjoy House for an Art Lover for its access to the work of the Mackintoshes, its sense of space, progression, volumes, intimacy and display, and not fret too much about the detail or become precious about the provenance.

CHECK WEBSITE FOR OPENING TIMES
NEARBY: 72 PALACE OF ART

The Millennium: 89–100

IN 1997 SCOTLAND voted for a Parliament with significant legislative powers which reconvened in Edinburgh in 1999, 292 years since it had voted itself out of existence. A growing sense of, and confidence in, a distinct Scottish cultural identity was given concrete expression in both a function and a building and in the fact that Edinburgh was now a genuine capital. This has had a profound effect on Scotland towards both international trends and personalities and its own cultural history. Internationally-renowned architects who have recently left their mark on Scotland include Norman Foster, Alfred Munkenbeck, Richard Rogers, Moshe Safdie, David Chipperfield, Kengo Kuma, Richard Meier, Eisaku Ushida, Zaha Hadid, Enric Miralles and Benedetta Tagliabue.

The corollary to this is an unforced response to Scottish architectural and cultural history, nothing like the self-conscious, self-referential and strenuous efforts of the 1930s and 1990s, and the results, inevitably, seem and are inevitable. The stress, strain and striving, while it might be present in preliminary notes and sketches, is entirely resolved in the finished works. At the same time, new ideas about Scottish architectural identity have emerged both in theory and practice and these ideas have themselves opened up architectural dialogues with Canadian and Japanese architects and resulted in a significant presence at the 2023 Venice Biennale.

Perhaps, above all it's the recovery of an indigenous Gaelic concept, *dùthchas,* which very loosely translates as heredity or patrimony but encompasses not merely the physical products of culture but the originating natural environment and climate and the gods, myths and legends connected to them.

Museum of Scotland from George IV Bridge

Museum of Scotland interior

Museum of Scotland
Chambers Street, Edinburgh, 1991–9

Architect
Benson + Forsyth

I'VE WRITTEN EXTENSIVELY elsewhere about this building so I'll confine myself to this.

My youngest grandchild calls it the 'old museum' partly because the NMS next door (see entry 37) was renovated when he was very young, thus becoming the 'new' museum, and partly because of how it looks both outside and in. He uses the same descriptions of it – 'castle', 'church' – as did the architectural commentators on its opening in 1999 and finds it as exciting, novel and quirky as any well-preserved ruin he's visited. From the basement vault containing Pictish stones and crosses to the rooftop viewing platform and its wild Scottish garden this building has embedded itself in his memory. He has his favourite places: the machine hall where we take a picnic lunch on the stepped lecture seats opposite the steam engine craned in before the roof was constructed; the historic Scottish landscapes in the basement with many of the formerly extinct species exhibited now being re-wilded; the lighthouse model; the many balconies that afford different viewpoints of every space; the great canyon that rises from basement to roof; the model of the pithead; the tiny turnpike stair in the rear corner of the building. I realise I'm also talking about my own likes.

Princely meddling, as happened at the National Gallery in London, which would have prevented all of this was thwarted; this is Scotland after all, and the Scottish people got the museum they richly deserved.

CHECK WEBSITE FOR OPENING TIMES
NEARBY: 20 GLADSTONE'S LAND
21 HERIOT'S HOSPITAL
38 NATIONAL MUSEUM
45 CENTRAL LIBRARY
64 NATIONAL WAR MEMORIAL
100 FUTURES INSTITUTE

DCA exterior

DCA interior

Dundee Contemporary Arts (DCA)
Nethergate, Dundee, 1999

90

Architects
Richard Murphy,
Richard Murphy Architects

ARTISTS, ACTORS AND musicians have always been drawn to marginal spaces where they might live, associate, practice, perform and display their work. Rents are cheap; properties are quirky and rambling and can be freely, even riskily, adapted at little cost; regulations are few and feebly administered; and a sense of supportive community can be engendered. These networks might circle around particular arts spaces. One thinks of the Tramway in Glasgow and Summerhall in Edinburgh. When the unofficial becomes official the risk is that that 'vibe', the very thing that made the artistic community work, can be lost.

The genius of the DCA, a spin-out of the Dundee Cultural Quarter, is that no such loss has occurred. The building, part new part converted, forms an L-shaped route where one transitions through box office, shop, cinema, exhibition space, café, restaurant, performance space and studios almost randomly and where the seemingly ad hoc and temporary physical means of its construction are made plain. Murphy's detailing is complex, layered, engaging, seemingly impermanent and insubstantial although not so and, like temporary backdrops and part-permeable scrims, creates the stage on which one can be part of, can be, the theatrical entertainment. There's a phrase we use in rock music: 'tight but loose'. That's the DCA.

CHECK WEBSITE FOR OPENING TIMES
NEARBY: 39 THE McMANUS
86 DUNDEE REP
97 V&A DUNDEE

Scottish Parliament from Arthur's Seat

Scottish Parliament Debating Chamber

The Scottish Parliament
Holyrood, Edinburgh, 1999–2004

Architects
Enric Miralles (1955–2000) and Bendetta Tagliabue (b.1963) of EMBT with RMJM as executive architects

FOR ALL THE initial furore about this building – the Catalan designers, the site, the costs, the design – it has been absorbed into Scottish culture and only a few curmudgeons still hold the negative view. It is a gathering place for the local, for the tourist, for the protester. My friend architect Neil Gillespie caught it best:

> It is a building we should know and understand. It evokes a landscape, a hyperborean landscape, a FINN land… It is about the glacier, in the crush of the folding of space and form. It is about the birch tree, the girl of the forest, given architectural form in the delicate screens to MSP offices. The concrete Canongate throws fragments of stone and drawing to its surface like some glacial moraine. It eschews passing beauty for something more profound and grounded in this territory. It is about a place beyond the restricted parochial boundaries of Scotland, it is located firmly in a northern territory. This is not an easy landscape, it is the chaos of the moraine, the anxiety of the gorge, the horror of the void, the silence of Munch's scream.

The Scottish Parliament is not the kind of building that suggests it would have appealed to Gillespie, whose architecture is cool, controlled and, on occasion, of an almost German *sachlichkeit*, but it was a measure of the building's catholicity and Gillespie's perceptiveness and generosity of spirit that it did.

BOOKING REQUIRED FOR CHAMBER
NEARBY: 78 CANONGATE HOUSING

Homes for the Future

Homes for the Future
Lanark Street, Glasgow, 2000

92

Architects
Elder & Cannon, McKeown Alexander (subsequently jm architects), Rick Mather, Ian Ritchie, RMJM, Ushida Finlay, Wren Rutherford ASL (subsequently Austin, Smith-Lord)

THE DEMONSTRATION PROJECT masterplan by Page \ Park confirmed they had knowledge of the Internationale Bauausstellung (IBA), Berlin, 1979–1987. IBA was an easily accessible urban workshop for Scottish architects, academics, students and developers in the mid to late 1980s through to the early 2000s.

In that context, as a response to late 20th-century inner urban Glasgow life rather than to an entirely speculative future home, the designs of Elder & Cannon, Rick Mather and Ian Ritchie show the greatest promise. They provide a perimeter frontage and contain the inner court of terrace and stand-alone blocks. Ritchie incorporated a genuine outside room which had the twin benefits of providing generous usable external space to each flat in a six-storey tenement while resolving the means of escape from a bedroom opening off the open-plan living room and kitchen.

These blocks reinterpreted the IBA investigation of public, private and semi-public/semi-private space while the stand-alone blocks within the landscaped court defined their own private/public relationship to the court and derived their form in part from the 'urban villa' apartment block that made its appearance at IBA.

PRIVATE DWELLING
NEARBY: 46 TEMPLETON'S

Pier Arts

Pier Arts
Victoria Street, Stromness, Orkney, 2007

Architect
Reiach & Hall

WHAT BECAME THE Pier Arts Centre was, in the 19th century, first the harbourside house of the local agent for the Hudson's Bay Company, then that of the owner of a fleet of herring boats. Following desultory uses in the first half of the 20th century it was acquired in 1977 by the Pier Art Centre Trust to house the initial 67 works of modern art donated by the Berlin-born communist, peace-activist and philanthropist Margaret Gardiner (1904–2005), then resident on Rousay, a principled, cultured and adventurous woman whose life as lived was in itself a history of the 20th-century avant-garde.

The building was converted to an art gallery in 1979 by Kate Heron and Axel Burrough to house 'one of the finest collections of the period in the UK' of works by Gardiner's friends, the modern British painters and sculptors such as Barbara Hepworth, Ben Nicholson, Naum Gabo, Eduardo Paolozzi, Wilhelmina Barns-Graham, Patrick Heron and Alfred Wallis among others.

The collection has been much expanded since such that a new wing of sympathetic form designed by Reiach & Hall, the so-called 'black house' for temporary exhibitions was added on the site of the former Hudson's Bay Company warehouse to complement the original, the 'strong house', which houses the expanded collection, now comprising 180 works of art.

CHECK WEBSITE FOR OPENING TIMES

Sandiefield

Sandiefield Housing
Crown Street, New Gorbals, Glasgow, 2010

Architect
Elder & Cannon

I HAVE SELECTED Sandiefield as emblematic of Glasgow's continuing dynamic revitalisation of gap sites in the 19th-century inner industrial suburbs now lacking the all-important industry and in the demolished mass housing projects of the 1960s. The New Gorbals is the site of the former Hutcheson E development, known variously as 'Hutchie E' or, with typical Glaswegian directness, 'the Dampies' due to its appalling condensation and mould problems. The domestic model of its replacement, although not the architecture, is the Scottish tenement with its particular attributes of community, security, human scale and urban presence.

This commanding corner block in a blue/black brick is an architecture of some subtlety. The windows are deep-set to emphasise the depth, solidity and presence of the brick walls and they are organised rigorously both vertically and horizontally to provide that sense of the infinite that Alexander Thomson wrote about. The wall is terminated by taller windows and a deep parapet which also reflects on Thomson's interest in 'proportion' and in the 'superincumbent mass' of the entablature supported by the columns or the wall below. The cleverness here is that the parapet/entablature masks a shallow monopitch roof which slopes away to the rear elevation. The balconies are, for once, genuine balconies large enough for effective use and the filigree framing of them lightens the elevation while at the same time, seemingly disengaged, extends across to tie in with the line of the adjacent block.

PRIVATE DWELLING

Murphy House

Murphy House
Hart Street, Edinburgh, 2015

Architect
Richard Murphy, Richard Murphy Architects

IN 2018, LONG before I visited Richard Murphy's house, I had been astounded by his remarkable 'Cabinet of Curiosities' exhibited at the Royal Scottish Academy (RSA). It was triangular in plan, each side holding six display recesses, each containing a 'curiosity', that could be concealed or exposed by means of precision-made cabinetry doors, screens and shelves. It was the very thing that an Edwardian gentleman would have had in his library as conversation piece.

His house is a cabinet of curiosities. It can be closed, as shown in this image, in an almost sombrely and soberly Japanese fashion with its metal and masonry interpretations of the less substantial *shoji* and *amado* screens, or open like a Californian beach villa on a cool autumn evening.

Internally also everything is either partially concealed like the stairs or a bath or can be closed up tight. Huge solid screens on counterweights and pulleys in the ceilings can cut off the rooflights and shutters shut off the windows, sealing the house up tight. Or those self-same screens and shutters can be thrown open, even the masonry quoins on the right are hinged; a winter house and a summer house. There's far more to this house and its intriguing section and levels where different actions or functions are allocated different locations in a spiralling route to ever more discrete and discreet locations.

PRIVATE DWELLING

NEARBY: 26 ROYAL HIGH SCHOOL
        58 RW FORSYTH'S

The Three Bridges from the north

The Three Bridges from the south

The Three Bridges

South Queensferry, Edinburgh and North Queensferry, Fife

> **Architects**
> Fowler & Baker, 1890
> Mott, Hay & Anderson, Freeman Fox, 1964
> Forth Crossing Bridge Constructors, Ramboll, 2017

IT'S NOT A building. It's not even three buildings. It's an engineering marvel of one bridge from each of the 19th, 20th and 21st centuries: a red rivetted cantilever for trains, a grey welded and wired steel suspension for cars, and a white concrete and steel cable-stay bridge for general traffic respectively. As an ensemble, it's unquestionably the most spectacular river crossing anywhere. An arrowhead into Fife and to the north. It's a place, a vast place, in that the outer bridges frame both North and South Queensferry and the river in between at the narrow point of the Firth of Forth. It draws Rosyth dockyard and one-time ferry terminal and the Hound Point oil terminal and cruise ship anchorage into its embrace. And since it's a place, it's included here.

Make sure to get a starboard window seat on your next flight to or port from Edinburgh airport. Take the train, take a bus, drive there. Sit outside a café or bar in either of the Queensferrys and marvel. Go on a North Sea cruise. Buy a ticket on the *Maid of the Forth* and sail from South Queensferry to Inch Colm and back again under all three bridges. Hope that the North Sea ferry route from Rosyth will be reinstated and that you may do likewise on your way to or from Den Haag or Esbjerg.

OPEN ALL YEAR ROUND

The V&A Dundee

Under the V&A Dundee

V&A Dundee
Riverside Esplanade, Dundee, 2018

97

Architect
Kengo Kuma (b.1954)

NEITHER THE LANDFALL Building, the Swimming Pool (both demolished late 20th century) or the still extant but diminutive Discovery Pavilion gave focus to Dundee Waterfront west of the Tay Road Bridge. Kuma's competition-winning V&A Dundee most certainly does.

I'm in two minds about this building. Its urban and place-making qualities aside, it's drafty outside and in. It opens to the west and the route beneath the building to the viewing point over the Tay estuary runs roughly east west, Kuma patently unaware of the Islander's wise prescription on orientation. The inverted pyramid containing the public spaces of entrance, café, shop and main stair sacrifices function for artifice. The finish inside and out is surprisingly rough, surprising, that is, until you read Kuma on the matter:

> I also strive to have this type of courage to break down and break away from the 'nice-looking' buildings of industrial society and create architecture that appears uneven and tarnished.

Nonetheless, although flawed, it's an important building, a significant addition to Dundee's cultural offer and it hosts some fabulous exhibitions beautifully presented. The permanent exhibition of Scottish Design is soon to be expanded.

CHECK WEBSITE FOR OPENING TIMES
NEARBY: 39 THE McMANUS
86 DUNDEE REP
90 DCA

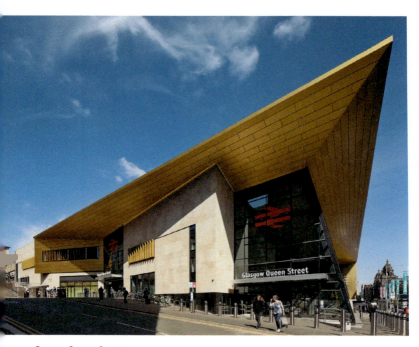

Queen Street Station

Queen Street Station

Queen Street, George Square, Glasgow, 2021

Architect
BDP

IN ALL THE many years and many times that I have travelled from Edinburgh Waverley to Glasgow Queen Street since my first time in 1966 on a drawing commission, to then studying at the Mackintosh School of Art, and to designing exhibitions in Stirling's Library (now GOMA), the Kelvingrove Art Gallery and Museum and a pavilion at the Glasgow Garden Festival, the exhilaration of being stood beneath that soaring single arched train shed roof quite evaporated on my being squeezed out into the Cathedral Street taxi rank or the service lane of Dundas Street or down those awkward steps at the vehicle drop off point on West George Street. This was no way to enter Scotland's largest city. Central Station did it so much better.

But now there is the great contrapuntal horizontal slash of a roof and a huge inclined window onto George Square with an oblique view of the City Chambers emphatically announcing to travellers that they have reached their destination. The station has been opened up both at the level of those buying tickets, waiting for trains and connecting between upper and lower stations and spatially (in the architectural sense) in that the great arch is given a new relevance. At the level of detail the security gates with their cutouts mimicking the arch and implying a distant Mackintosh connection are a clever touch and the use of gold anodising throughout is joyous. This is exactly how one wants to arrive from the East!

OPEN ALL YEAR ROUND

NEARBY: 32 ST VINCENT ST. CHURCH
50 ST VINCENT CHAMBERS
54 WILLOW TEA ROOMS
56 LION CHAMBERS

Simon Square Housing

Simon Square Housing
Howden Street, Edinburgh, 2022

Architect
Fraser Livingstone Architects

MALCOLM FRASER OF Fraser Livingstone has written about a 'new Scottish urban vernacular' based on his experience designing this tiny, but significant, four-storey tenement, consisting of six one and two-bedroom flats and duplexes, in the heterogenous context of Howden Street.

Before considering the more general matter of an urban vernacularism there are some points to be made about the plan and construction of the building itself. The skewed plan is determined, especially on the west and to the south elevations, by overlooking constraints which have then been developed as an overall aesthetic.

The tenement is constructed throughout – walls, floors and roof – from cross-laminated timber (CLT), sometimes known as mass timber construction, which forms the structure that supports insulation and brickwork. The bricks are 'slaistered' (Scotland has a unique building lexicon), that is, given a thin mortar coating which provides a pleasing irregularity and tactility

Virtually all the newness of this building is hidden behind the brickwork. Flat roof aside, it presents volumetrically, in whiteness with paratactical fenestration all of which signify a Scottish vernacular, urban or rural, devised either from the untutored necessity of the occasional builder or intellectually conceived by the architect as here. It would be intriguing to see how Fraser Livingstone might translate the lessons of this little jewel into something larger.

PRIVATE DWELLING

NEARBY: 21 HERIOT'S HOSPITAL
38 NATIONAL MUSEUM
89 MUSEUM OF SCOTLAND
100 FUTURES INSTITUTE

The Edinburgh Futures Institute, interior

Edinburgh Futures Institute
(formerly Edinburgh Royal Infirmary)
University of Edinburgh, Lauriston Place, 1870–79

100

Architect
1870–79, David Bryce and
2020–24, Bennetts Associates

THE MOST RELIABLE future is the one predicated on the development, not the recreation, of the past. In utilising the former Infirmary the Edinburgh Futures Institute does precisely that. Moreover, existing buildings, where practically adaptable, are our present-day greatest constructional resource. They incorporate personal capital, cultural capital, financial capital and the environmental capital of embodied carbon.

Those who visited when it was a bustling hospital will recognise its broad stairs, wide, wide corridors and airy wards now transformed to free-flowing multi-purpose use while all can enjoy the substantial reinstatement of original masonry, timber, lead, ironwork and plaster detailing and marvel at the numerous retained donor and ward boards throughout. It is against such positive restoration that Bennett Associates have placed their respectful but robustly and elegantly crafted and stunningly coloured interventions of new linking blocks, new stairs, new lifts and adapted the original spaces to new uses. In addition, the University has demystified its functions by bringing large parts of the Edinburgh Futures Institute into public use.

I began with a house older than the pyramids; I merely pause five thousand years later with a promise for the future.

CHECK WEBSITE FOR OPENING TIMES
NEARBY: 20 GLADSTONE'S LAND
21 HERIOT'S HOSPITAL
38 NATIONAL MUSEUM
45 CENTRAL LIBRARY
88 MUSEUM OF SCOTLAND

Timeline

Date	World	Scotland
3180 BCE		Skara Brae
3000 BCE	Sumerian cuneiform writing	
2800 BCE		Maes Howe
2630 BCE	Saqqara Pyramid	
2600–2500 BCE	Giza Pyramids	
2500 BCE		**Calanais Circle**
		Tomnaverie Circle
2500–2000 BCE		**Ring of Brodgar**
1500–1001 BCE	First Chinese dictionary	
1200 BCE	Epic of Gilgamesh	
1193 BCE	Destruction of Troy	
900 BCE		Celts arrive in Scotland
753 BCE	Rome founded	
600–500 BCE	Mayans appear in Mexico	
500–200 BCE		**Broch of Gurness**
pre 400 BCE	Olmecs in Mesoamerica use a version of the 'zero'	
43 BCE	Roman invasion of England	
80–850 CE		Pictish culture
122 CE		Hadrian's Wall
142 CE		Antonine's Wall
180 CE		Romans defeated
360 CE		Scots and Picts invade England
410 CE	Romans quit Britain	

543 CE		Possible founding of Glasgow
610 CE		Edinburgh founded
843 CE		Kenneth MacAlpin first king of Picts and Scots
927 CE	Aethelstan first king of England	
1040	Moveable type printing in China	
1044	First report of invention of gunpowder in China	
1066	Norman invasion of England	
1100	St Germain-des-Près, Paris The Gothic period	
1124		First Scottish coinage Edinburgh becomes Royal Burgh
1137		**St Magnus Cathedral**
ca.1170		Glasgow becomes royal burgh
1179		Aberdeen chartered
1191		Dundee becomes royal burgh
1204		**Dirleton Castle**
1215	Magna Carta	
1260–70		**Caerlaverock Castle**
1260	Cimabue paints 'Trinità Madonna'	
1265–1308		John Duns Scotus, Scottish philosopher
1271–95	Marco Polo in China	

TIMELINE

ca. 1250–1650	Hanseatic League, North and Baltic Seas trade	
ca. 1280		**Lochranza Castle**
1296–1357		Wars of Independence
1307–21	Dante's Divine Comedy	
1315		Battle of Bannockburn
1320		Declaration of Arbroath
1346–53	Black Death throughout Europe	
ca. 1380		**Crichton Castle**
		St Machar's Cathedral
1411		St Andrews University founded
1412	Brunelleschi's 'Rules of Perspective' The Renaissance	
1446		**Rosslyn Chapel**
1448–64	Anglo–Scot wars	
1451		Glasgow University founded
1453	Guttenberg prints the Mazarin bible	
1467		Scottish Parliament bans 'fute-ball and golfe'
1472		Norway cedes Orkney, Shetland and Nan Eilean Siar to Scotland
1492	Columbus discovers the Bahamas and Cuba	
1495		Aberdeen University founded
1503	da Vinci's 'Mona Lisa'	

1512	Copernicus states Earth orbits the Sun	
1530–1722		**Tankerness House**
1550–1617		John Napier, inventor of logarithms
1564–1616	William Shakespeare, playwright	
1582		Edinburgh University founded
ca. 1580		**Claypotts Castle**
1595		**Kirbuster Farmhouse**
1603		Union of Crowns of Scotland and England
	King James I of England and VI of Scotland	
1610–26		**Craigievar Castle**
1616	Galileo banned by Vatican from further scientific work	
1617–21		**Gladstone's Land**
ca. 1620		**The Study, Culross**
		Lamb's House
1628–93		George **Heriot's School**
1633–1868	Japan closes its borders, the *sakoku* period	
1642–51	English Civil War	Cromwell invades Scotland
1649–60	The Commonwealth, a brief British republic	
1707		Union of Parliaments at Westminster
1709 and 1715		First Jacobite rebellions

TIMELINE

1711–76		David Hume, Scottish philosopher
1745		Second Jacobite Rebellion
1746		Battle of Culloden
ca. 1750–1830		The Enlightenment
1753		**Gunsgreen House**
1757–73		**Paxton House**
1759–96		Robert Burns, poet
1765		James Watt's steam engine
1766		James Craig's plan for Edinburgh New Town
1770		**Inveraray**
1771–1832		Sir Walter Scott, novelist
1775–83	American War of Independence	
1789	French Revolution	
1804–15	Napoleonic Wars	
1805–12		**Stobo Castle**
1825–9		**Royal High School**
1837–99	Queen Victoria on throne The Victorian era	
1846–59		**Balfour Castle**
1849		**Cathedral of the Isles**
1851	The Great Exhibition, Paxton's Crystal Palace	
1853–56	Crimean War	
1853–92		**The Blackhouse**
1855–6		**Gardner's Warehouse**
1857–9		**Holmwood** **St Vincent St. Church**

1860		**Lammerburn**
1861		**Barclay Bruntsfield Church**
	Unification of Italy	
1862		**Wallace Monument**
1863–73		**Kibble Palace**
1864		**Grove Street Tenement**
		National Museum
1865		**The McManus**
		Grecian Chambers
	Unification of Germany	
	Franco–Prussian War	
1872		First international football match, held Glasgow: Scotland and England draw 0–0
1875		**Mortuary Chapel**
1876	First telephone call	
1879–81		**Queen's Cross Church**
1880–81	First Boer War in South Africa	
1881–6, 1907–30		**St Conan's Church**
1883	Krakatoa eruption	
1885		**John Morgan House**
1887–90, 1901–3		**Edinburgh Central Library**
1889, 1936		**Templeton's**
1889–93		**Kirkton Cottages**
1893–1901		**Mansfield Traquair**
1898	Marie Curie discovers radium	
1898–1900		**Melsetter House**
1899–1902		**St Vincent Chambers**
1900–4		**The Daily Record**

TIMELINE

1902–4		The Hill House
1903–6		St John Evangelist
1903		Willow Tea Rooms
	First heavier-than-air flight by Wright Brothers	
1904		Riselaw House
1905		Lion Chambers
1906–7		St Peter's RC Church
1906–7, 1923–5		RW Forsyth's
1907		Duke Street Halls
1907, 1979		John Paris Shop
1909		Artist's Studio
1911		Grangewells
1911, 1936		The Hippodrome
1914–18	First World War	
1917	Russian Revolution	
1919	Spanish Flu epidemic	
1924–7		Scottish National War Memorial
1926	General Strike in Britain	
1929	Wall Street Crash, Depression	
1929–33		Reid Memorial Church
1931–45	Japan invades Manchuria	
1933	Adolf Hitler becomes German Chancellor	
1933–9		St Andrew's House
1934		The Lane House
1934		Dunfermline Fire Station
1935–6		Jenners Flats

Year	Event	Building
1936		*Queen Mary* launched on River Clyde
1936–8	Spanish Civil War	
1937–53		**Kirkcaldy Town House**
1938		Glasgow Empire Exhibition
		Palace of Art
		St Peter-in-Chains
		Rothesay Pavilion
1939–45	Second World War	
1942–4		**Italian Chapel**
1945	Atom bomb dropped on Hiroshima and Nagasaki	
1947	Indian Independence, partition into India and Pakistan	
		Edinburgh International Festival founded
1947–9	Jackson Pollock 'drip' paintings	
1947–51		**Pitlochry Dam**
1948	Creation of the National Health Service	
1948–52		**Telephone Exchange**
1950–3	Korean War	
1951	Festival of Britain	
1954	JRR Tolkien's *Lord of the Rings*	
1955–65	Vietnam War	
1956–8		**St Paul's RC Church**
1956	Suez Crisis	
	USSR invades Hungary	
1961	East Germans erect the Berlin Wall	
1961–9		**Canongate Housing**

TIMELINE

Year	Event	Building
1962	Beatles release 'Love Me Do', Beatlemania	Sillitto House
1963–5		Gala Fairydean
1963–7		Cumbernauld Town Centre
1963–8		St Andrew's University Halls of Residence
1966–76	Cultural Revolution in China	
1967	'Summer of Love', San Francisco	
1968	'Prague Spring' USSR invades Czechoslovakia Woodstock Festival	Edenside Medical Practice
1969	Apollo Moon landing	
1971–84		The Burrell Collection
1973	Oil Crisis, 'Three-day week' in United Kingdom	
1973–6		Eden Court Theatre
1976	Milton Friedman and monetarism	
1982		Dundee Rep
1984–9		21st Century Tenement
1984–5	Miners strike throughout the UK	
1987	Black Monday financial crash	
1988		House for an Art Lover
1989–91	Berlin wall falls. USSR collapses. New nation-states.	
1990	Hubble telescope launched into low-Earth orbit	
1991–9		Museum of Scotland

1991	UK financial recession	
1992	Francis Fukuyama's *The End of History* published	
1997		Devolution Referendum won
1999		**DCA**
1999–2004		**Scottish Parliament**
2000		**Homes for the Future**
2004	Tsunami in South East Asia	
2007		**Pier Gallery**
2009	Worldwide financial crash	
2010		**Sandiefield Housing**
2012	Higgs' 'boson' discovered at CERN in Geneva	
2014		Independence Referendum lost
2015		**Murphy House**
2017		**The Three Bridges**
2018		**The V&A Dundee**
2020–2	Coronavirus pandemic	
2021	James Webb space telescope launched	
		Queen Street Station
2022		**Simon Square Housing**
	Russia invades Ukraine	
2023	Gaza conflict	
2024		**The Edinburgh Futures Institute**

Glossary

Amsterdam School	the loose group of architects working in and around Amsterdam in the 1910s and '20s in a highly distinctive Expressionistic brick architecture.
ashlar	hewn blocks of stone with flat polished faces and straight arrises (edges).
Art Deco	the art, architecture and product design of the prevailing style exhibited at the Exposition International des Arts Décoratifs et Industriels Moderne held in Paris 1925.
Baroque	a Classical style with an emphasis on dramatic fluid composition and striking, tending towards massive, masonry detailing and startling natural lighting effects.
Beaux-Arts	the school of architecture in Paris teaching a very specific method of Classical architecture where design is a staged linear process.
bed	the horizontal mortar joint between bricks or stones in masonry construction. See perpend.
bedding-plane	how sedimentary rocks are laid down as sediment over time in distinct bands separated by other geologic events. This gives rise to thick bedding planes as was the case at the Craigleith quarry that supplied Edinburgh's stone or thin bedding planes as at Walliwall.
big toon	a term to describe the urban characteristics of Aberdeen, Dundee, Edinburgh, Glasgow, Inverness and Perth.
box-bed	a fully enclosed timber bed with doors rather like a large cupboard.
Brutalism	an architectural style where concrete is used expressively straight from the shuttering (the mould) with no further finish applied. From the French *béton brut*, 'raw concrete'.
Cailleach na Mointeach	Old Woman of the Moors (anglicised as Cailleach), significant topography suggestive of the female form.
Classicism	the architecture derived from the models of ancient Greece and Rome.
corbel, corbelling	the horizontal projection of one or more successive courses of stone or brick to support a cornice, balcony or to create a vault.

corbel table	a continuous projecting range of masonry supported by corbels.
Diocletian window	an arched window split into three panes by square mullions. Derived from the windows in the Diocletian Thermae (Baths) in Rome. Sometimes known as a Thermal Window.
dúthchas	Gaelic: heredity or patrimony but encompassing humankind, the land, the sky and the gods and their interaction. Cf. Martin Heidegger *das Geviert*, the Fourfold.
embodied carbon	the quantity of carbon already produced from mineral extraction, material processing, product fabrication, construction and energy use and waste production in the creation of an existing building and consequently not adding further construction-generated carbon emissions.
Expressionism	the conscious identification and exaggeration of the parts of the building which demonstrates the interaction of architectural form as dynamic and expressive of movement. A subset of Modernism. Also written as expressionismus.
Free-style	a loose descriptor to cover the work of the exponents of a freer Art & Crafts architecture such as Philip Webb, WR Lethaby, CFA Voysey and ES Prior. Often shown as English Free-style.
genius loci	the rather nebulous 'spirit of the place'. A term popularised by the Norwegian theorist Christian Norberg-Schulz.
gesamptkunstswerk	the total work of art where all the parts – the architecture, the furnishings, the fitments, the artwork, even the accompanying music and books – are of a unity; a Modernist ideal derived from the German Romantic poets and Richard Wagner.
Gothicism	the architecture of the twelfth to the sixteenth centuries, identifiable by the use of the pointed arch.
harl(ing)	From Scots 'to drag'. Lime or cement render over brick or rubble stone.
Hanseatic League	a North and Baltic Sea trading collective of the twelfth to seventeenth centuries.
Hennebique	Francois Hennebique (1842–1921). First used steel-reinforced concrete in 1879, obtaining patents for his system in 1892.
hygroscopic	the property of a substance to absorb moisture from adjoining substances.
Jugendstil	the 'young style', German Art Nouveau, more rectilinear than its French and Belgian counterparts.

GLOSSARY

ligne-claire	a distinctive single-line drawing style initiated by Georges Rémi (Hergé) and perpetuated by his studio and assistants.
Lord Provost	the senior politician in a Scottish burgh, equivalent to an English mayor.
low road	the route of the dead. The song 'The Bonnie Banks o' Loch Lomond' references taking both high road and low road, by sweetheart and her deceased lover respectively, whereby they come to Loch Lomond. He, being in the spirit world, arrives soonest.
Mannerism	a highly stylised and extreme version of any architectural style. A particular late Renaissance architectural style associated with Michaelangelo and Serlio.
Modernism	the anti-aesthetic and ahistorical architecture that developed in France, Germany, the Netherlands, Scandinavia and Czechoslovakia immediately post-WWI.
National Romanticism	a late 19th and early 20th-century architectural style particular to Finland and, to an extent, Sweden and the Baltic States which featured massive construction, mostly in granite, and stylised decoration drawn from folk tradition and from nature.
Neo-Classicism	essentially, new-Classicism where the strict rules derived from Greek and Roman precedent are ignored, adapted, transformed or perverted.
(the) Orders	the dimensionally and decoratively defined system of increasing elaboration of Classical architecture: the Doric, the Ionic and the Corinthian to which the Romans added the Tuscan between the Doric and Ionic and the Composite, a mash up of the Ionic and Corinthian, after the Corinthian.
Palladian	a sophisticated, symmetricised architectural style developed by the Venetian architect Andrea Palladio (1508–80) and widely published in his *Quattro Libri*.
parametric(al)	non-symmetrical, non-regular architectural composition.
paratactic(al)	non-symmetrical, non-regular but balanced detail.
perpend	the vertical mortar joint between bricks or stones in masonry construction. See bed.
piano nobile	the principal floor of a Classical building, usually the first floor and identified by the tallest and most decorative windows.
pilaster	flat-sided column flush or projecting marginally from the adjacent wall.
pylon	a ceremonial gateway in Egyptian architecture of massive form and distinctive battered (sloped) sides.

SCOTLAND IN 100 BUILDINGS

Renaissance	the recovery of Classical culture in the late fourteenth and early fifteenth-century Italy and its subsequent spread throughout Europe.
rock-faced	masonry blocks so carved as to give the impression of being rough-hewn from the quarry or found as fieldstone.
Rococo	a light frothy Classical style of a complex three-dimensional form enlivened by exuberant plasterwork often coloured white and gilt.
Rogue-Gothic	a catch-all descriptor to cover those 19th-century architects who didn't follow the precise precepts of Gothic.
Romanesque/Norman	a relatively plain architectural style that predates the Gothic in the tenth to the 12th centuries (and later in Scotland) identifiable by its use of the rounded arch.
sachlichkeit	sometimes shown as the *neue sachlichkeit*, the 'new objectivity', a rational functionalist form of Modernism.
Secession or Sezession	artists' groups which rejected the very restrictive requirements on exhibiting promulgated by the 19th-century European Art Academies
Serlio	Sebastiano Serlio (1475–1554), Italian Mannerist architect, author of *I Sette Libri dell'Architettura*. Inventor of the Serliano, a tripartite window where the central opening is arched and supported on two Tuscan columns which also carry the flat lintels of the flanking windows to their respective jambs.
skewputt	the bottom-most stone of a gable designed to prevent the other coping stones ('skews' in Scots) from sliding off.
slaistering/slaistered	a thin mortar coating over masonry construction; roughly comparable to English 'parging'.
sma burgh	a term differentiating the urban characteristics of the smaller Scottish town, such as Haddington, Stromness, Ullapool etc., from those of the cities, the big toons.
standstill moon	every 18.6 years, for about a year, the moon's cycle is such that it rises and sets very far south and then two weeks later rises and sets very far north. At Calanais the moon appears to graze the horizon. There is an optical illusion which makes it appear huge.
Staple	a Scottish trading enclave based in a foreign port.
Star Trek	the design of the seating, in particular the speaker's chair, in the aborted parliamentary debating hall in the Royal High School was of such a particularly futuristic aspect that the chamber became known locally as the Star Trek flight deck.

GLOSSARY

stoa	a covered colonnade in Greek architecture.
tea chute	a large, vertical store for tea.
Term or Herm	a Grecian boundary marker comprising a tapered post surmounted by a head and shoulders of the god Hermes. Generally such a statue featuring any symbolic personage.
trilithon	the stone post-and-lintel structures forming part of a henge.
Tuscan	a more elaborated and refined form of the Doric order. A Roman invention.
voussoir	a wedge-shaped stone that forms part of an arch.
Walliwall	is named for a quarry just to the west of Kirkwall although the thin-bed stone is found throughout the archipelago. 'Wall' is from the Norse *vagr* meaning 'bay'. Kirkwall, *kirkju vagr*, is the bay of the church.
Zeno narrative	the Zeno family were wealthy Venetian seafarers of the late fourteenth century who may have ventured across the Atlantic to what is now North America and acted as pilots to the Sinclair family on a similar expedition.

Bibliography

Alison, Archibald, *Essays on the Nature and Principles of Taste* (4th ed) (Edinburgh, 1815)

Allan, John, and Duncan Macmillan, *The Museum of Scotland: Benson + Forsyth* (London, 2000)

Architectural Heritage Society for Scotland, *Architectural Heritage III: The Age of Mackintosh* (Edinburgh, 1992)

Barley, Nick (ed), *Homes for the Future* (London, 1999)

Bilcliffe, Roger, *Mackintosh Watercolour* (London, 1978)

____, *Charles Rennie Mackintosh: The Complete Furniture, Furniture Drawings and Interior Designs* (2nd ed) (Guildford and London, 1980)

Billings, Robert William, *The Baronial and Ecclesiastical Antiquities of Scotland*, (4 vols) (Vol. 1) (Edinburgh, 1847–52)

Blackie & Son, *Villa and Cottage Architecture: Select examples of country and suburban residences recently erected; with a full descriptive notice of each building* (London, 1868)

Boardman, Philip, *The Worlds of Patrick Geddes: Biologist, Town Planner, Re-educator, Peace-Warrior* (London, 1978)

Bonnar, Thomas, *Biographical Sketch of George Meikle Kemp* (Edinburgh, 1892)

Brennan-Inglis, Janet, *Scotland's Castles: Rescued, Rebuilt and Reoccupied* (Stroud, 2014)

Buchan, James, *Capital of the Mind: How Edinburgh Changed the World* (London, 2003)

Buchanan, William (ed), *Mackintosh's Masterwork: The Glasgow School of Art* (Glasgow, 1989)

Burnet, Sir John, Tait and Lorne, *The Information Book of Sir John Burnet, Tait and Lorne* (London, 1934)

Calder, Alan, *James McLaren: Arts & Crafts Pioneer* (Donnington, 2003)

Campbell, Ian, 'A Romanesque Revival and the Early Renaissance in Scotland c.1380–1513', *Journal of the Society of Architectural Historians*, Vol. 54, No. 3, September 1995

Clarke, DV, TG Cowie and Andrew Foxon (eds), *Symbols of Power: At the Time of Stonehenge* (Edinburgh, 1985)

Cooper, Jackie (ed), *Mackintosh Architecture* (London, 1984)

Crawford, Robert, *On Glasgow and Edinburgh* (Cambridge MA, 2013)

Curl, James Stevens, *Victorian Architecture* (Newton Abbot, 1990)

Curtis, William J R, *Modern Architecture Since 1900* (2nd ed) (Oxford, 1987)

Daiches, David, Peter Jones and Jean Jones, *A Hotbed of Genius: The Scottish Enlightenment 1730–1790* (Edinburgh, 1986)

Dakin, Anthony, Miles Glendinning and Aonghus MacKechnie (eds), *Scotland's Castle Culture* (Edinburgh, 2011)

Dorward, David, *Scotland's Place-names* (Edinburgh, 1995)

Edwards, Brian, *Basil Spence, 1907–1976* (Edinburgh, 1995)

Ekelund, Hilding (trans Edward Birse), *Architecture in Finland* (Helsinki, 1932)

Emmerson, Roger, *Winners & Losers: Scotland and the Architectural Competition* (Edinburgh, 1991)

____ and Daniela Karasová, Petr Krajčí and Radomíra Sedláková, *Prague 1891–1941* (Edinburgh, 1994)

____, 'The Emperor's New Clothes: Pastiche and Reproduction', *Architectural Heritage VI* (Edinburgh, 1996)

____, '(P/T)owerplay: A reading of national authority in architecture', *292:Essays in Visual Culture* (Edinburgh, 2000)

____ and Mary Tilmouth, *Matt Steele Architect: A Biography* (Edinburgh, 2010)

____, 'Circumnavigating the Globe: RW Forsyth's, Princes Street, and its meanings', *The Book of the Old Edinburgh Club*, New Series, Vol. 16 (Edinburgh, 2020)

____, *Land of Stone: a journey through modern architecture in Scotland* (Edinburgh, 2022)

_____, 'Dam-nation: Benevean Dam, Lawers Dam, Megget Dam', *Alder* (Dunkeld, 2023)

Empire Exhibition, *Official Guide* (Glasgow, 1938)

_____, *Illustrated Souvenir of the Palace of Arts* (Glasgow, 1938)

Ferguson, William, *The Identity of the Scottish Nation* (Edinburgh, 1998)

Fergusson, James, *An historical inquiry into the true principles of beauty in art, more especially with reference to architecture* (London, 1849)

_____, *History of Architecture in All Countries from the Earliest Times to the Present Day* (2 vols) Vol. 1 (New York, 1867)

_____, and Robert Kerr, *History of Modern Styles of Architecture* (3rd ed) (London, 1891)

Fiddes, Valerie, and Alastair Rowan (eds), *Mr David Bryce* (Edinburgh, 1976)

Frampton, Kenneth, *Modern Architecture: a Critical History* (4th ed) (London, 2007)

Frew, John, and David Jones (eds), *Scotland and Europe: Architecture and Design 1850–1940* (St Andrews, 1991)

Garnham, Trevor, *Melsetter House, William Richard Lethaby* (London, 1993)

Gifford, John, *The Buildings of Scotland: Fife* (London, 1999)

Gillespie, Neil, and Laura Kinnaird (eds), *Stravaigers* (Edinburgh, 2015)

Glendinning, Miles, Ranald MacInnes and Aonghus MacKechnie, *A History of Scottish Architecture: From the Renaissance to the Present Day* (Edinburgh, 1996)

_____, and Diane Watters (eds), *Home Builders: Mactaggart & Mickel and the Scottish housebuilding industry* (Edinburgh, 1999)

_____, *The Architecture of Scottish Government: From Kingship to Parliamentary Democracy* (Dundee, 2004)

_____, *Modern Architect: The Life and Times of Robert Matthew* (London, 2008)

_____, and Aonghus MacKechnie, *Scotch Baronial: Architecture and*

National Identity in Scotland (London, 2021)

Gomme, Andor, and David Walker, *Architecture of Glasgow* (London, 1968)

Groenendijk, Paul, Piet Vollard and Han van Dijk, *Guide to Modern Architecture in the Netherlands* (Rotterdam, 1987)

Hausen, Marika, Kirmo Mikkola, Anna-Lisa Amberg, and Tytti Valton (eds), *Eliel Saarinen, Projects, 1896–1923* (Cambridge MA, 1990)

Herman, Arthur, *The Scottish Enlightenment: The Scots' Invention of the Modern World* (London, 2002)

Howard, Jeremy, *Art Nouveau: International and National Styles in Europe* (Manchester, 1996)

Jackson, Neil, *Peter Womersley* (Liverpool, 2023)

Kallir, Jane, *Viennese Design and the Wiener Werkstätte* (London, 1986)

Kimura Hiroaki, 'Charles Rennie Mackintosh', *Process*, No. 50, August 1984

Kinchin, Perilla and Juliet Kinchin with J Neil Baxter, *Glasgow's Great Exhibitions: 1888, 1901, 1911, 1938, 1988* (Bicester, n.d., ca. 1988)

Kivinen, Paula, Pekka Korvenmaa, and Esa Piironen (eds), *Lars Sonck, 1870–1956, Architect* (Helsinki, n.d.)

Kleihues, Josef P, and Heinrich Klotz (eds), *The International Building Exhibition Berlin, 1987: Examples of a New Architecture* (London, 1987)

Klein, Shiela, *The See-Through House: My Father in Full Colour* (London, 2021)

Langmead, Donald, *Willem Marinus Dudok, A Dutch Modernist: A Bio-Bibliography* (Westport CT, 1996)

Lethaby, WR, *Architecture, Mysticism and Myth* (London, 1891)

_____, *Architecture* (London, 1911)

Long, Philip, and Jane Thomas, *Basil Spence Architect* (Edinburgh, 2007)

Lynch, Michael, *Scotland: A New History* (London, 1992)

McAra, Duncan, *Sir James Gowans: Romantic Rationalist* (Edinburgh, 1975)

McArthur, Alexander, and H Kingsley Long, *No Mean City* (London, 1943)

MacDiarmid, Hugh, *Aesthetics in Scotland* (Edinburgh, 1984)

McFadzean, Ronald, *The Life and Work of Alexander Thomson* (London, 1979)

MacGibbon, David, and Thomas Ross, *The Castellated and Domestic Architecture of Scotland from the Twelfth to the Eighteenth Century* (5 vols) (Edinburgh, 1887)

McHardy, Stuart, *Scotland's Future History* (Edinburgh, 2015)

____, *Scotland's Future Culture* (Edinburgh, 2017)

McKean, Charles, *The Scottish Thirties* (Edinburgh, 1987)

____, *The Making of the Museum of Scotland* (Edinburgh, 2000)

McKinstry, Sam, *Rowand Anderson: 'The Premier Architect of Scotland'* (Edinburgh, 1991)

MacLeod, Robert, *Style and Society: Architectural Ideology in Britain 1835–1914* (London, 1971)

____, *Charles Rennie Mackintosh: Architect and Artist* (London, 1983)

MacRae, EJ, *The Heritage of Greater Edinburgh* (Edinburgh, 1947)

Markus, Thomas A (ed), *Order and Space in Society* (Edinburgh, 1982)

Maudlin, Daniel, *The Highland House Transformed: Architecture and Identity on the Edge of Britain, 1700–1850* (Dundee, 2009)

Moffat, Alexander, and David Riach, *Arts of Independence* (Edinburgh, 2014)

Moffat, Alistair, *Remembering Charles Rennie Mackintosh* (Lanark, 1989)

Moon, Karen, *George Walton: Designer and Architect* (Oxford, 1993)

Morris, Eleanor, *James Morris: Architect and Landscape Architect, 1931–2006* (Edinburgh, 2007)

Murphy, Richard, *Of Its Time and Place: The Work of Richard Murphy Architects* (London, 2012)

Muthesius, Herman (trans Janet Seligman and Stewart Spencer), *The English House: Volume 1 Development* (London, 2007) (orig. Berlin, 1906)

Naismith, Robert, *The Buildings of the Scottish Countryside* (London, 1985)

Nikula, Riitta, *Armas Lindgren, 1874–1929, Architect* (Helsinki, 1988)

____, *Architecture and Landscape: The Building of Finland* (Helsinki, 1993)

Normand, Tom, *The Modern Scot: Modernism and Nationalism in Scotland 1928–1955* (London, 2000)

Nuttgens, Patrick, *Reginald Fairlie 1883–1952: A Scottish Architect* (Edinburgh, 1959)

____ (ed), *Mackintosh and His Contemporaries* (London, 1988)

O'Donnell, Raymond, *James Salmon 1873–1924* (Edinburgh, 2003)

Paavilainen, Simo (ed), *Nordic Classicism 1910–1930* (Helsinki, 1982)

Payne, Peter, *The Hydro: Study of the Development of the Major Hydro-electric Schemes Undertaken by the North of Scotland Hydroelectric Board* (Aberdeen, 1988)

Pevsner, Nikolaus, *Pioneers of Modern Design* (Harmondsworth, 1966)

____, and JM Richards, *The Anti-Rationalists* (London, 1973)

Phillips, R Randall, *Houses for Moderate Means* (London, 1936)

Plummer, Henry, *Nordic Light: Modern Scandinavian Architecture* (London, 2012)

Reiach, Alan, and Robert Hurd, *Building Scotland: A Cautionary Guide* (Glasgow, n.d., ca. 1944)

Ringbom, Sixten, *Stone, Style and Truth* (Helsinki, 1987)

Robb, Steven, 'Ebenezer MacRae and Interwar Housing in Edinburgh', in RJ Morris (ed), *The Book of the Old Edinburgh Club*, New Series, Vol. 13, 2017

Robertson, Pamela (ed), *Charles Rennie Mackintosh: The Architectural Papers* (Cambridge MA, 1990)

Rock, Joe, *Thomas Hamilton Architect 1784–1858* (Edinburgh, 1984)

Rodger, Johnny, *The Hero Building: An Architecture of Scottish National Identity* (Farnham, 2015)

____ (ed), *Gillespie, Kidd & Coia: Architecture 1956–1987* (Glasgow, 2007)

Rodger, Richard, *Housing the People: the Colonies of Edinburgh* (Edinburgh, 1999)

Rosenburg, Lou, with John Rosser, *Scotland's Homes Fit for Heroes: Garden City Influences on the Development of Scottish Working Class Housing 1900–1939* (Edinburgh, 2016)

Ruskin, John, *Lectures on Architecture and Painting Delivered at Edinburgh, November 1853* (London, 1854)

Russell, Frank (ed), *Art Nouveau Architecture* (London, 1979)

Savage, Peter, *Lorimer and the Edinburgh Craft Designers* (Edinburgh, 1980)

Scottish Housing Advisory Committee, *Planning Our New Homes* (Edinburgh, 1944)

Service, Alastair, *Edwardian Architecture* (London, 1977)

Sinclair, Fiona, *Scotstyle: 150 Years of Scottish Architecture* (Edinburgh, 1984)

____, and Neil Baxter (eds), *Scotstyle: 100 Years of Scottish Architecture (1916–2015)* (Edinburgh, 2016)

Smith, George Gregory, *Scottish Literature: Character and Influences* (London, 1919)

Stamp, Gavin, 'Mackintosh, Burnet and Modernity', in *Architectural Heritage III: The Age of Mackintosh* (Edinburgh, 1992)

____, and Sam McKinstry (eds), *'Greek' Thomson* (Edinburgh, 1994)

____, *Alexander Thomson: The Unknown Genius* (London, 1999)

____ (ed), *The Light of Beauty and Truth: The Lectures of Alexander 'Greek' Thomson Architect 1817–1875* (Glasgow, 1999)

Stewart, John, *The Life and Works of Glasgow Architects: James Miller and John James Burnet* (Dunbeath, 2021)

Tonge, John, *The Arts of Scotland* (London, 1938)

Ushida Findlay and Michael J Ostwald, 'Ushida Findlay' in *2G: Revista Internacional de Arquitectura* No. 6 (Barcelona, 1998),

Vergo, Peter, *Art in Vienna, 1898–1918* (2nd ed) (Oxford, 1981)

Walker, David M, *St Andrew's House: An Edinburgh Controversy 1912–1939* (Edinburgh, 1989)

Walker, Frank Arneil, 'National Romanticism and the Architecture of the City', in George Gordon (ed), *Perspectives of the Scottish City* (Aberdeen, 1985)

____, 'The Significance of the Folk House', in John Frew and David Jones (eds), *Scotland and Europe: Architecture and Design 1850–1940* (St Andrews, 1991)

____, *Mousa to Mackintosh: The Scottishness of Scottish Architecture* (Edinburgh, 2023)

Welter, Volker M, *Biopolis: Patrick Geddes and the City of Life* (Cambridge MA, 2002)

Weston, Richard, *Richard Murphy: Ten Years of Practice* (Edinburgh, 2001)

Wilson, Peter, *New Timber Architecture in Scotland,* (Edinburgh, 2007)

Young, Andrew McLaren, *Charles Rennie Mackintosh (1868–1928): Architecture, Design and Painting* (Edinburgh, 1968)

Illustration Credits

Unless otherwise attributed, all drawings and photographs
are the copyright of Roger Emmerson.

Page 16	Skara Brae by Museum, own work; https://commons.wikimedia.org/wiki/File:Orkn_Skara_Brae.jpg; CC BY-SA 3.0 Unported License.
Page 18	Above: Maes Howe and the mountains of Hoy by Bill Broaden; https://www.geograph.org.uk/photo/3638228; CC BY-SA 2.0 Generic License.
Page 20	Above: Standing Stones of Calanais by Peter Moore; https://geograph.org.uk/photo/4311296; CC BY-SA2.0 License.
Page 22	Above: Tomnaverie Standing Stones by Neill Williamson; https://commons.wikimedia.org/wiki/File:Tomnaverie_Stone_Circle_(3394819192).jpg; CC BY-SA 2.0 Generic License.
Page 24	Ring of Brodgar by Liberaler Humanist; https://commons.wikimedia.org/wiki/File:Ring_of_Brodgar,_Photo_9,_10.08.2015.jpg; CC BY-SA 3.0 Unported License.
Page 26	Above: Broch of Gurness in Summer by Chmee2, own work; https://commons.wikimedia.org/wiki/File:Broch_of_Gurness_in_Summer_2012_(22).jpg; CC BY_SA 3.0 Unported, 2.5 Generic, 2.0 Generic, 1.0 Generic Licenses; also on front cover, cropped.
Page 30	Above: St Magnus Kathedrale Orkney by Warndernder Weltreisender; https://commons.wikimedia.org/wiki/File:St._Magnus_KathedraleOrkney.jpg; CC BY-SA 3.0 Unported License. Below (bottom cropped to fit): St Magnus Cathedral-nave by Gordon Hatton; https://commons.wikimedia.org/wiki/File:St_Magnus_Cathedral_-_nave_-_geograph.org.uk_-_6901711.jpg; CC BY-SA 20 Generic License.
Page 32	Above: Dirleton Castle by Richard Sutcliffe; https://commons.wikimedia.org/wiki/File:Dirleton_Castle_-_geograph.org.uk_-_4854305.jpg; CCBY-SA 2.0 Generic License (also on back cover, cropped). Below: The Cellars in Dirleton Castle by Deepsphotography, own work; https://commons.wikimedia.org/wiki/File:The_Cellars_in_Dirleton_Castle_jpg; CC BY-SA 3.0 Unported License.
Page 34	Above (top cropped to fit): Caerlaverock Castle by Orikrin 1998, own work; https://commons.wikimedia.org/wiki/File:Caerlaverock_castle.jpg; CC BY-SA Unported License. Below: Caerlaverock Castle courtyard by Billie McCrorie; https://www.geograph.org.uk/photo/4064306.jpg;

SCOTLAND IN 100 BUILDINGS

CC BY-SA 2.0 Generic License.

Page 36	Lochranza Castle, Isle of Arran by Arran_Bee, https://commons.wikimedia.org/wiki/File:Lochranza_Castle,_Isle_of_Arran_-_Flickr_-_Arran_Bee.jpg; CC BY-SA 2.0 License.
Page 38	Above: Crichton Castle by Tom Parnell; https://commons.wikimedia.org/wiki/File:Crichton_Castle_(2476323408).jpg; CC BY-2.0 Generic License. Below: Crichton Castle by Prussianblues, own work; https://commons.wikimedia.org/wiki/File:Crichton_Castle.jpg; CC BY-SA 3.0 Unported.
Page 40	St Machar's Cathedral, Old Aberdeen by Alan Findlay; https://commons.wikimedia.org/wiki/File:St_Machar%27s_Cathedral,_Old_Aberdeen_-_geograph.org.uk_-_2638325.jpg; CC BY-SA 2.0 Generic License.
Page 42	Rosslyn Chapel by Thomas Duesing (bottom cropped to fit); https://commons.wikimedia.org/wiki/File:Rosslyn_Chapel_(457060628).jp; CC BY-A 2.0 Generic License.
Page 44	Above: Kirbuster Farm Museum by Andrew Riley; https://www.geograph.org.uk/photo/5837477.jpg; CC BY-SA 2.0 Generic License. Below (bottom cropped to fit): Kirbuster Farm Museum, Orkney by Nick McNeill. https://commons.wikimedia.org/wiki/File:Kirbuster_Farm_Museum,_Orkney_-_geograph.org.uk_-_2216418.jpg; CC BY-SA 2.0 Generic License.
Page 46	Dundee, Claypotts Castle by PaulT (Gunther Tschuch) own work (sides cropped to fit); https://commons.wikimedia.org/wiki/File:Dundee_Claypotts_Castle_03.jpg; CC BY-SA 4.0 International License.
Page 48	Kirkwall, Tankerness House Museum Entrance by Ymblanter, own work; https://commons.wikimedia.org/wiki/File:Kirkwall_Tankerness_Hoiuse_Museum_Entrance.jpg; CC BY-SA 4.0 International License.
Page 50	Culross – The Study by Colin Park (top cropped to fit); https://commons.wikimedia.org/wiki/File:Culross_-_The_Study_NTS_-_geograph.org.uk_-_6484959.jpg; ; CC BY-SA 2.0 Generic License.
Page 56	Craigievar Castle facing the entrance by Alan Stokes; https://commons.wikimedia.org/wiki/File:Craigievar_Castle_facing_the_entrance.jpg; CC BY-SA 4.0 International License (also on back cover, cropped).
Page 58	Gladstone's Land by Tony Hisgett; https://commons.wikimedia.org/wiki/File:Gladstones_Land_(4530213293).jpg; CC BY-A 2.0 Generic License.
Page 60	Above: George Heriot's and the Old Infirmary from Edinburgh Castle by Kim Traynor; https://commons.wikimedia.org/wiki/File:George_Heriot%27s_and_the_Old_Infirmary_from_Edinburgh_Castle_-_geograph.org.uk_-_2179684.jpg; CC BY-SA Generic License.

ILLUSTRATION CREDITS

Below: Public Domain.

Page 62 — Inveraray by Holger Uwe Schmitt (top cropped to fit); https://commons.wikimedia.org/wiki/File:1743_wurde_damit_begonnen_Inveraray_als_Planstadt_neu_erbauen_03.jpg; CC BY-SA 4.0 International License.

Page 64 — Gunsgreen House by Gordon Yuill (left side cropped to fit); https://commons.wikimedia.org/wiki/File:Gunsgreen_House_-_geograph.org.uk_-_1857387.jpg; CC BY-SA 2.0 Generic License.

Page 66 — Above: Front of Paxton House by Stephen Craven; https://commons.wikimedia.org/wiki/File:Front_of_Paxton_House_-_geograph.org.uk_-_5910894.jpg; CC BY-SA 2.0 Generic License (cropped to fit). Below: Entrance to Paxton House by Jim Barton; https://commons.wikimedia.org/wiki/File:Entrance_to_Paxton_House_-_geograph.org.uk_-_5746843.jpg; CC BY-SA2.0 Generic License.

Page 68 — Above (bottom cropped to fit): Stobo Castle by Rosser 1954 Roger Griffith; https://commons.wikimedia.org/wiki/File:Stobo_Castle,_Scottish_Borders.jpg; Public Domain. Below: Public Domain.

Page 74 — Balfour Castle and Doocot by Ronnie Deas; https://commons.wikimedia.org/wiki/File:Balfour_Castle_%26_Doocot_Shapinsay_Orkney.jpg; CC BY-SA 4.0 International License.

Page 78 — Above: Arnol Blackhouse by PaulT (Gunther Tschuch); https://commons.wikimedia.org/wiki/File:Arnol_Blackhouse_02.jpg; CC BY-SA 4.0 International License. Below: Arnol Blackhouse inside by Urbanplay, own work: https://commons.wikimedia.org/wiki/File:Arnol_Bkackhouse_inside.jpg; CC BY-SA 3.0 Unported License.

Page 82 — Above: Holmwood House by Derek Rankine; https://commons.wikimedia.org/wiki/File:Holmwood_House_(4847654846).jpg; CC BY-SA 2.0 Generic License. Below: Holmwood cupola and chimeraae, Glasgow Scotland by Rosser 1954, own work; https://commons.wikimedia.org/wiki/File:Holmwood_cupola_and_chimeraae,_Glasgow,_Scotland.jpg; CC BY-SA 4.0 International License.

Page 84 — Above: St Vincent Street Free Church by Steve Cadman; https://commons.wikimedia.org/wiki/File:StVincentStreetFreeChurch.jpg; CC BY-SA 2.0 Generic License (cropped to fit). Below: St Vincent Street Free Church interior by Wee Holly, own work; https://commons.wikimedia.org/wiki/File:05374_UP-UF-St_Vincent_St_Pa_Spirit_Free_Church,_Blythswood_021.jpg; CC BY-SA 4.0 International License.

Page 90 — Wallace Monument by dun_deagh; https://commons.wikimedia.org/wiki/File:Wallace_Monument_From_Stirling_Castle_(5897934336).jpg; CC BY-SA 2.0 Generic License.

Page 92 — Above: Kibble Palace by LornaMCampbell, own work; https://commons.wikimedia.org/wiki/

	File:Glasgow_-_703_Great_Western_Road,_Botanic _Gardens,_Kibble_Palace_-_20160407155121.jpg; CC BY-SA 4.0 International License. Below: Kibble Palace, glazing detail by Alex Livet; https://commons.wikimedia.org/wiki/File:Kibble_Palace_(30022885395).jpg; CC-CCO 1.0 Universal Public Domain Dedication.
Page 98	Dundee - McManus Galleries Building by Colin Park: https://commons.wikimedia.org/wiki/File:Dunde_-_McManus_Galleries_Building_-_geograph.org.uk_-_5231397.jpg; CC BY-SA 2.0 Generic License.
Page 102	Mortuary Chapel, Arbroath by Tom Parnell, own work; https://commons.wikimedia.org/wiki/File:Allen-Fraser_Mortuary_Chapel_-_view_from_NW.jpg; CC BY-SA 4.0 International License.
Page 106	Above (bottom cropped to fit): St Conan's Kirk by Tom Parnell; https://commons.wikimedia.org/wiki/File:St_Conan%27s_Kirk_(22703587007).jpg. CC BY-SA 2.0 Generic License. Below: Nave and Chancel, St Conan's Kirk by Stuart Wilding: https://commons.wikimedia.org/wiki/File:Nave_and_Chancel,_St_Conan%27s_Kirk_-_geograph.org.uk_-_4138447.jpg; CC BY-SA 2.0 Generic License.
Page 110	Central Library by Brian McNeill (bottom cropped to fit): https://commons.wikimedia.org/wiki/File:Central_Library_Edinburgh_pano3.jpg; CC BY-SA 3.0 Unported License.
Page 112	Above (top and bottom cropped to fit): Templeton's carpet factory by Spike, own work; https://commons.wikimedia.org/wiki/File:Glasgow_Templeton_On_The_Gree_01.jpg; CC BY-SA 4.0 International License (also on front cover, cropped). Below: Carpet factory by Anthony O'Neill; https://commons.wikimedia.org/wiki/File:carpet_factory_-_geograph.org.uk_-_4108034.jpg; CC BY-SA 2.0 Generic License.
Page 116	Mansfield Traquair Centre by Alasdair W, own work; https://commons.wikimedia.org/wiki/File:City_of_Edinburgh_-_Catholic_Apostolic_Church_-_20230924122415.jpg; CC BY-SA 4.0 International.
Page 124	The Hill House by Tom Parnell; https://commons.wikimedia.org/wiki/File:The_Hill_House,_Helensburgh_-_view_through_boundary_wall,_from_W.jpg; CC BY-SA 4.0 International License.
Page 126	The Daily Record printing works by Jean-François Capdehttps://commons.wikimedia.org/wiki/File:The_Daily_Record_Printing_Works_in_Renfield_Lane_-_panoramio.jpg; CC BY-A 3.0 Unported License.
Page 130	The Willow Tea Rooms by JJC Marshall, own work; https://commons.wikimedia.org/wiki/File:Mackintosh_At_The-Willow.jpg; CC BY-SA 4.0 International.
Page 134	Lion Chambers by Stinglehammer, own work (bottom cropped to fit): https://commons.wikimedia.org/wiki/

ILLUSTRATION CREDITS

	File:172_Hope_Street,_Lion_Chsmbers_01.jpg; CC BY-SA 4.0 International License.
Page 148	Above: Hippodrome by Magnus Hagdorn; https://commons.wikimedia.org/wiki/File:Hippodrome_(51370676926).jpg; CC BY-SA -2.0 Generic License.
Page 152	Above: Scottish National War Memorial by Osama Shukir Muhammed Amin FRCP (Glasg); https://commons.wikimedia.org/wiki/File:The_façade_of_the_Scottish_National_War_Memorial,_Edinburgh_Castle,_Scotland.jpg; CC BY-SA 4.0 International License. Below: The Scottish National War Memorial by Alan Findlay; https://commons.wikimedia.org/wiki/File:The_Scottish_National_War_Memorial,_Edinburgh_Castle_-_geograph.org.uk_-_2472577.jpg; CC BY-SA 2.0 Generic License.
Page 156	Below: St Andrew's House by Alan Ford; https://commons.wikimedia.org/wiki/File:StAndrewsHouse-Edinburgh.jpg. CC BY-SA 2.0 Generic License.
Page 160	Dunfermline Fire Station by Tom Parnell (bottom cropped to fit): https://commons.wikimedia.org/wiki/File:Fire_Station,_Carnegie_Drive,_Dunfermline.jpg; CC BY-SA 4.0 International License.
Page 164	Below (sides cropped to fit): Kirkcaldy Town House clock by Kenhare, own work; https://commons.wikimedia.org/wiki/File:Kirkcaldy_Town_House%27s_rather_fine_clock_tower.jpg; CC BY-CC0 1.0 Universal Public Domain Dedication;
Page 166	Above (top and bottom cropped to fit, image levelled): Pavilion, Argyle Street, Rothesay by Leslie Barrie; https://commons.wikimedia.org/wiki/File:Pavilion,_Argyle_Street,_Rothesay_-_geograph.org.uk_-_3071987.jpg; CC BY-SA 2.0 Generic License. Below: Rothesay Pavilion by Ian Paterson; https://commons.wikimedia.org/wiki/File:Rothesay_Pavilion_-_geograph.org.uk_-_3990018.jpg; CC BY-SA 2.0 Generic License.
Page 168	Above: Palace of Art by LornaMCampbell; https://commons.wikimedia.org/wiki/File:Palace_of_Art,_Bellahouston_Park,_Glasgow,_4.jpg; CC BY-SA 4.0 International License. Below: Palace of Art by Lorna M Campbell; https://commons.wikimedia.org/wiki/File:Palace_of_Art,_Bellahouston_Park,_Glasgow,_1.jpg; CC BY-SA 4.0 International License.
Page 170	St Peter-in-Chains, Ardrossan by Leslie Barrie (sides cropped to fit); https://St_Peter-in-Chains,_Ardrossan_-_geograph.org.uk_-_3379274.jpg; CC BY-SA 2.0 Generic License.
Page 172	Above: Italian Chapel, Orkney by Vidario, own work; https://commons.wikimedia.org/wiki/File:Italian_Chapel_orkney.jpg. CC BY-SA 3.0 Unported License. Below: Italian Chapel interior by D Brooke 1829, own work. https://commons.wikimedia.org/wiki/

	File:Orkney_Islands_-_Italian_Chapel_-_20160715114042.jpg; CC BY-SA 4.0 International License.
Page 176	Pitlochry dam and power station by Andrew Abbott; https://commons.wikimedia.org/wiki/File:Pitlochry_dam_and_power_station_-_geograph.org.uk_-_3206021.jpg; CC BY-SA 2.0 Generic License.
Page 180	Above: St Paul's RC Church, Glenrothes by Michael Westwater (Mcwesty), own work; https://commons.wikimedia.org/wiki/File:St_Pauls_RC_Church_Glenrothes.jpg; CC BY-SA 3.0 Unported License. Below left: St Paul's RC Church interior by Tom Parnell; https://commons.wikimedia.org/wiki/File:St_Paul%27s_RC_Church,_Glenrothes_(291791777).jpg; CC BY-SA 2.0 Generic License. Below right: St Paul's RC Church interior by Tom Parnell; https://commons.wikimedia.org/wiki/File:St_Paul%27s_RC_Church,_Glenrothes_(291791725).jpg; CC BY-SA 2.0 Generic License.
Page 188	Above: Andrew Melville Hall by Tom Parnell; https://commons.wikimedia.org/wiki/File:Andrew_Melville_Hall_(5860500969).jpg; CC BY-SA 2.0 Generic License. Below: Andrew Melville Hall by Tom Parnell; https://commons.wikimedia.org/wiki/File:Andrew_Melville_Hall_(5861054024).jpg; CC BY-SA 2.0 Generic License.
Page 190	Above: Cumbernauld Town Centre Building by Ross Watson; https://commons.wikimedia.org/wiki/File:Cumbernauld_Town_Centre_building_-_geograph.org.uk_-_3585279.jpg; CC BY-SA 2.0 Generic License. Below: Cumbernauld Town Centre by Edinburgh College of Art; https://commons.wikimedia.org/wiki/File:Tower_Block_UK_photo_cl1-58.jpg; CC BY-SA 4.0 International License.
Page 192	Below: Edenside Medical Group, Kelso, plan, Neil Jackson.
Page 194	Above: Burrell Collection by Ardfern, own work; https://commons.wikimedia.org/wiki/File:Burrell_Collection,_June_2012_(01).jpg; CC BY-SA 3.0 Unported License. Below: Burrell Collection interior by JoeDerrySetch, own work; https://commons.wikimedia.org/wiki/File:Burrell_Collection_Interior_6_2022.jpg; CC BY-SA 4.0 International License.
Page 196	Above (top cropped to fit): Eden Court Theatre by Andrew Abbott; https://commons.wikimedia.org/wiki/File:Eden_Court_Theatre_(geograph_3205858).jpg; CC BY-SA 2.0 Generic License. Below: Eden Court Theatre detail by Tom Parnell; https://commons.wikimedia.org/wiki/File:Eden_Court_(514034615).jpg; CC BY-SA 2.0 Generic License.
Page 202	Above: Peace Cairn and House for an Art Lover by Barbara Carr; https://commons.wikimedia.org/wiki/File:Peace_Cairn_and_House_for_an_Art_Lover_-_grograph. org.uk_-_3454616.jpg; CC BY-SA 2.0 Generic License. Below: House for an Art Lover, Bellahouston Park, Glasgow by wfmillar; https://commons.wikimedia.org/wiki/

ILLUSTRATION CREDITS

	File:House_for_an_Art_Lover,_Bellahouston_Park,_Glasgow_-_geograph.org.uk_-_2089913.jpg; CC BY-SA Generic License (also on front cover, cropped).
Page 206	Below (bottom cropped to fit): National Museum of Scotland interior by Irid Escent; https://commons.wikimedia.org/wiki/File:National_Museum_of_Scotland_20171206_113031_(49364039442).jpg; CC BY-SA 2.0 Generic License.
Page 210	Below: Scottish Parliament Debating Chamber by Colin: User/Wikimedia Commons CC BY-SA 4.0; https://commons.wikimedia.org/wiki/File:Scottish_Parliament_Debating_Chamber_3.jpg; CC BY-SA 4.0 International License.
Page 214	Pier Arts, Stromness, Orkney. Gavin Fraser FOTO MA.
Page 220	Above: Bridges over the River Forth by Mike McBey; https://commons.wikimedia.org/wiki/File:Bridges_over_the_River_Forth_(40130096735).jpg; CC BY-SA 2.0 Generic License. Below: The Firth of Forth and its Bridges by MJ Richardson; https://commons.wikimedia.org/wiki/File:The_Firth-of_Forth_and_its_bridges_(geograph_5831088).jpg; CC BY-SA Generic License.
Page 222	Above: V&A, Dundee by Richard Szwejkowski; https://commons.wikimedia.org/wiki/File:Dundee_1190419_103.jpg; CC BY-SA 2.0 Generic License. Below: The V&A Museum, Dundee by MJ Richardson; https://commons.wikimedia.org/wiki/File:The_V%5EA_Museum,_Dundee_-_geograph.org.uk_-_5914848.jpg; CC BY-SA 2.0 Generic License.
Page 224	Queen Street Station, Glasgow. BDP, also on back cover, cropped.

Acknowledgements

I AM INDEBTED TO: Gavin MacDougall whose idea it was; Jennie Renton and Madeleine Mankey for convincing me how it could be done; the superb team at Luath Press: Amy Turnbull, Kira Dowie and Scott Kemp who saw it through to fruition; Stuart McHardy for invaluable access to his mythogeographic studies; all previous writers on Scottish architecture for the detail I often lacked; Peter Wilson, Roy Milne and Derek Fraser for decades-long debate and encouragement; Shweta Balasubramoni for her penetrating 'foreign gaze'; Laura Maginnis for her enthusiastic support; Neil Gillespie, a fellow-stravaiger; the late Gavin Stamp for providing access to many Alexander Thomson buildings (far more than are shown in this book); Richard Ewing for access to the Lane House; Mary Tilmouth for access to Grangewells; the Inspector for Art in Scottish Schools for access to St Andrew's House; the late Bertie Hornung for access to the Jenners flats; Richard Murphy for access to his house; Dr Christine Emmerson for access to the Edinburgh Futures Institute; the many churchwardens and helpers for access to the many churches discussed; clients Steven Winyard, and the Arcadia Group who allowed me to work on their A-listed buildings; Neil Jackson for permission to use the Edenside plan; Edward Dymock at BDP for permission to use the Glasgow Queen Street Station photograph; Gavin Fraser at FOTO MA for permission to use the Pier Arts Centre photograph; and, above all, as always, to my wife Chris.

Index

Names of buildings described in this book are in bold.

21st Century Tenement *200, 201*
3DReid, architects 139

Aberdeen 12, 91
    Canada House 109
    Hamilton Place 109
    Marischal College 109
    Northern Insurance 109
Aberdeen Philosophical Society 109
Aberdeen, Ruskin Society of 109
Aberdeen Senate, debating society 109
Adam, James, architect 55, 65, 67
    John, architect 55, 63, 67
    Robert, architect 55, 67
    William, architect 55, 63
Adam, John, and Alison Primrose, householders 51
Alberti, Leon Battista, artist/architect 55
Alford 12
Alison, Archibald, priest and essayist 101
American Institute of Architects
    RS Reynolds Memorial Award for Community Architecture 191
Anderson, Sir Robert Rowand, architect 117
Andrew Melville Hall *188, 189*
Andreson, Brit, architect 195
Arbroath 12
    Hospitalfield 103
Ardrossan 12
Artist's Studio *144, 145*
Arup, Ove, engineer 187
Australia
    Sydney Opera House 187
Austria
    Purkersdorf Sanatorium 127
Ayr 91
Ayton, William, architect 61

Baikie family, landowners 49
Baikie, William, benefactor 111
Baird 1, John, architect 81
Balcanquhall, Walter, Presbyterian minister 61
Balfour Castle, Shapinsay 31, *74, 75*
Barclay Bruntsfield Church *88, 89*
Baronial architecture 71, 91
Barns-Graham, Wilhelmina, artist, 215
BDP, architect 225
Bemersyde nr Melrose 91
Bennetts Associates, architect 229
Benson + Forsyth, architect 207
Berwick on Tweed, 3
Bexhill-on-Sea
    De La Warr Pavilion 167
Billings, Robert William, architectural illustrator 71, 75, 91, 103, 115
biplane with folding wings 68, 69
Black, William, solicitor 135
Blackhouse, The, Lewis *78, 79*
Blackie, Professor John Stuart, scholar 89
Blake, William, artist 117
Bogardus, James, architect 81
Bo'ness 12,
Boswell, George, architect 113
Boucher, James, architect 93
Boyd, John, iron-founder 93
Breuer, Marcel, architect 185
Brodgar, Ring of *24, 25*
Brown, Dan, author
Brown, Sir George Washington, architect 111
Bruce, Robert the, King of Scots 37
Bruce, Sir George, industrialist, 51
Bruce, Sir William, architect 55
Brunelleschi, Filippo, artist/architect 55
Bryce, David, architect 75, 229
Buchan, John (Lord Tweedsmuir), author and MP 157
Burn, William, architect 75
Burnet, Sir John James, architect 139
Burns, Robert, poet 91

263

Burrell Collection *194*, **195**
Burrell, Sir William, benefactor 195
Butterfield, William, architect 77

Caerlaverock Castle 12
Caesar, Julius 15
Cadell, William 'Bill', architect 143
calendar house 75
Calanais, Standing Stones *20*, **21**
Cambridge School 195
Cameron, Charles, architect 55
Campbell, Caroline, heiress 107
Campbell, Colen, architect 55
Campbell, John, 5th Duke of Argyll 63
Campbell, Walter Douglas, designer 107
Canongate Housing *182*, *183*, **193**
Čapek, Karel, playwright 59
Carlyle, Thomas, essayist and philosopher 109
Carnegie, Andrew, benefactor 111
Carr, David, architect 165
Carrick, James, architect 167
    James Andrew, architect 167
Central Library *110*, **111**
Chermayeff, Serge, architect 167
Chiocchetti, Dominico, artisan 173
Chipperfield, David, architect 205
Claypotts Castle *46*, **47**
Clyne, Arthur, architect 105
Coia, Jack, architect 171
Copcutt, Geoffrey, architect 191
Coulport 93
Cousland, James, architect 93
Covenanters 35
Craigievar Castle *56*, *57*, *71*, **125**
Cranston, Catherine, restaurateuse, 131
Crawford, Hunter, architect 119
Crichton Castle *12*, *38*, *39*, **71**
Crieff
    Innerpeffray Chapel 111
Cromwell, Oliver, Protector 33, 37
Culross 12,
    Abbey, monks of 51
    Moat mine 51

Cumbernauld 12
Cumbernauld Development Corporation 191
Cumbernauld Town Centre *190*, **191**
Curl, James Stevens, architectural historian 77
Cursiter, Stanley, painter 49

Daily Record Printing Works *126*, **127**
David I, King of Scots 33
De Brandt, Princess Sophie 67
De Klerk, Michel, architect 125
De Moor, Bob, strip-cartoonist 37
Denmark
    Helsingør, Kronberg Castle 61
designlab, architects 69
Demarco, Richard, artist and arts entrepreneur 73
Denmark
    Esbjerg 221
De Vaux, John, knight 33
Dey, William, architect 161
Dickson, Louis, cinema-owner 149
Dirleton Castle *12*, *32*, *33*, **39**
Dobson, Bennet, architect 133
Donegal Tunnelling Tigers, 177
Dryburgh Abbey 91
Dudok, Wilem Marinus, architect 157, 161, 167
Dundee 12, 47
    Cultural Quarter 199, 209
    Discovery Centre 223
    Tay Road Bridge 223
Dundee Contemporary Arts (DCA) *208*, **209**
Dundee Repertory Theatre *198*, **199**
Dunfermline 12
    Abbey 31
    Library 161
Dunfermline Fire Station *160*, **161**
Dunn & Watson, architects 115
Duke Street Church Halls *146*, **147**
Durham Cathedral 31

Eden Court Theatre *196*, **197**
Edenside Medical Practice *192*, **193**
Edinburgh 12
   Castle Terrace 87
   Chessels Court 183
   City Art Centre 163
   Colinton Road 87
   Cramond, Avisfield 185
   Flodden Wall 61
   Grange Park House 159
   Greenbank Terrace 145
   Hollister, George Street 139
   Hospital for Sick Children, Sciennes 117
   Meuse Lane 139
   Mortonhall Crematorium 197
   National Gallery of Scotland 117
   National Library of Scotland extension 197
   St Giles Cathedral 91
   St Mary's Cathedral 117
   Scottish Widows 197
   Summerhall 209
   Wester General Hospital, Nuffield Transplant Unit 187
Edinburgh Architectural Association 115
Edinburgh College of Art 179
Edinburgh Futures Institute, The **228**, **229**
Egypt, pyramids 15
   pylon 73
Eilean Donan 37, 213
Elder & Cannon, architects 167, 213, 217
Elgin 59
Elliot, Archibald, architect 69
Elliot, James, architect 69
Eyemouth 12

Falkirk Council 143, 149
Farrer, James, amateur archaeologist 19
Finland
   Helsinki 143
   Tampere 143
   Turku 143
Finnish National Romanticism 41, 105, 143, 147
Firth of Forth 51
Forbes, Mansfield, architectural historian 55
Forbes, William, merchant 57
Forth Crossing Bridge Constructors, engineer 221
Fortingall 12
Foster, Norman, architect 205
Fountainbridge Tenement *94*, **93**
Foulzie, Gilbert, protestant minister 49
Fowke, Captain Francis, architect 97
Fowler & Baker, engineer 221
France 15
   Bourges, House of Jacques de Coeur 49
   Paris 39
      Boulevard des Capucines 149
Franck, James Ernest, architect 161
Fraser, Elizabeth, heiress 103
Fraser Livingstone, architect 227
Fraser, Malcolm, architect 227
Fraser, Patrick Allan, designer 103
Frederick the Great, King of Prussia 67
Freeman Fox, engineer 221

Gabo, Naum, artist 215
Gala Fairydean Stadium *186*, **187**
Galashiels 12
   High Sunderland 187
Gardner's Warehouse *80*, **81**
Gardiner, Margaret, philanthropist 215
Gasson, Barrie, architect 195
Gaudí Antoni, architect 123
George Heriot's School *60*, **61**
German Expressionism 159, 167, 179
Germany
   Berlin 67
      Kottbusser Dam 127
      Universum Cinema 149

Hamburg, Rathaus 99
Internationale Bauaustellung 213
Leipzig University 67
Potsdam, Gardener's Cottage 83
Gibb, Sir Alexander, & Co., engineer, 177
Gibbs, James, architect 55
Gillespie, John Gaff, architect 135
Gillespie, Neil, architect 211
Gladstone's Land 58, 59
Glasgow 12
    Central Station 225
    Centre for Contemporary Arts 101
    City Chambers 225
    Craigie Hall 203
    Glasgow Herald Building 115
    GOMA 225
    Great Storm of 1968 201
    Kelvingrove Art Gallery & Museum 225
    Kelvinside, University 99
    Moray Place 201
    New Gorbals 217
    Pollok Country Park 195
    Scotland Street School 201
    Tramway 209
    Trongate, City Bank 91
Glasgow Arts Club 135
Glasgow Girls 119
Glasgow Garden Festival 225
Glasgow Institute of Architects 115
Glasgow School 119, 147
Glasgow School of Art 181
Gledstanes, Thomas and Bessie Cunningham, landowners 59
Glenrothes 12
Gordon, James, mapmaker 61
Gordon, John Graham, architect 133
Gothic architecture 29
Gowan, James, architect 189
Gowans, Sir James, architect 87
Grangemouth
    Avon Hall 115
Grangewells 146, 147
Grecian Chambers 100, 101

Greece
    Athens, Hephaisteion 73
    Parthenon 73
    Propylaea 73
    stoa 73
Greenock
    St Patrick's RC Church 171
Guild of St George, antiquarian society 109
Gunsgreen House 64, 65
Gurness, Broch of 26, 27

Haden, Thomas, decorative metalworker 137
Hadid, Zaha, architect 205
Hannesdottir, Kristen and Nick Groves-Raines, architect 53
Hamilton, Thomas, architect 73
Hanseatic League 53
Helensburgh 12
Hennebique system 135
Hepworth, Barbara, artist 215
Hergé (Georges Rémi) strip-cartoonist 37
Heriot, George, goldsmith and moneylender 61
Heron, Kate & Axel Burrough, architect 215
Heron, Patrick, artist 215
Highland Park 45
Hill House 124, 125
Hippodrome 148, 149
Hoffmann, Josef, architect 127
Holmwood 82, 83
Homes for the Future 212, 213
Hornung, Berthold 'Bertie', planner 163
Hoskins Associates, architect 97
House for an Art Lover 125, 202, 203
Howard, William Frederick, architect 165
Hudson's Bay Company 215
Hume,   George, landowner 67
    Ninian, plantation owner 67

INDEX

Patrick, landowner 67
Hurd, Robert, architect 163
Hurd, Robert & Partners, architect 53

Inveraray 12, 62, 63
Inverness 12
Israel
    Jerusalem, Temple on the Mount 43
Ireland 15
Irvine 89
Irving, Edward, minister 117
Italian Chapel 172, 173
Italy
    Ferrara, Palazzo Diamanti 39
    Venice, St Marks 31
    Venice Biennale 2023 205
    Verona, Palazzo Canossa 39
    Palazzo Diamanti 39
    Palazzo Pompei 39

James IV, King of Scots 37, 51, 61
Japan
    amado external screen 219
    Metabolist Group 191
    shoji internal screen 219
Jenners Flats 162, 163
John Morgan House 108, 109
John Paris Building 142, 143
Johnson, James Marr, architect 141
Johnson, Marcus, architect 161
Johnson, Philip 185
Johnson, Tom, Secretary of State for Scotland 177

Kahn, Louis I, architect, 57, 185, 193
Kelso 12, 89
Kibble Palace 92, 93
Kibble, John, inventor 93
Kilmacolm
    Windy Hill 159
Kininmonth, Willam, architect 159
Kirbuster Farm Museum 44, 45
Kirkcaldy Town House 164, 165
Kirkcaldy 12

Kirkton Cottages 114, 115
Kirkwall
    Free Library 111
Kramer, Piet, architect 125
Kropholler, Alexander, architect 171
Kuma Kengo, architect 205, 223

Lamb, Andro or Andrew, merchant 53
Lamb's House 52, 53
Lammerburn 86, 87
Lane House, The 158, 159
L'Art Decoratif, French design magazine 123
Law & Dunbar Naismith, architect, 197
Le Corbusier, architect 57, 169, 181, 193
Leiper, William, architect 113
Lethaby, William Richard, architect 119, 121
Lewis 12, 21, 189
Library Association of the United Kingdom 111
Lindberg, Hugo, architect 41, 105
Lindgren, Armas, architect 41, 105, 147
Linlithgow Palace 61
Lion Chambers 134, 135
Liverpool
    Oriel Chambers 81
    Anglican Cathedral 129
Lochawe 12
Lochnagar, 23
Lochranza Castle 12 , 36, 37
London 111
    Brent Town Hall 165
    bus 15
    All Saints Church, Margaret Street 77
    Hornsey Town Hall 165
    National Gallery, Sainsbury Wing 207
    Royal Albert Hall 97
    V&A 97
    Waltham Forest Town Hall 165
Lorimer, Sir Robert, architect 115,

119, 137, 153, 155
Lumière Frères, pioneer cinematographers 149

McAslan, John, & Partners, architect 195
McRae, Ken, architect 201
McConnell, Robert, iron-founder 81
McGibbon and Ross, architectural historians and illustrators 115
McGurn, Duncan, Logan & Opfer, architect 201
McHarg, Ian, landscape architect 185
McKean, Charles, architectural historian 57
McKeown Alexander (jm architects), architect 213
Mackintosh, Charles Rennie, architect 57, 85, 115, 119, 121, 125, 127, 129, 131, 147, 159, 181, 193, 201, 203, 225
Mackintosh, Margaret MacDonald, artist 117, 119, 203
Mackintosh School of Architecture 181, 201
MacLaren, John Marjoribanks, architect 115
McManus Art Gallery & Museum 98, 99
MacMillan, Andy, architect 181, 201, 203
MacNair, Frances MacDonald, artist 117, 119
MacNair, Herbert, artist 117, 119
MacPherson, James, author 15
Maes Howe 18, 19
MV *Maid of the Forth*
Mansfield Traquair Centre 116, 117
Mary, Queen of Scots, 53
Mather, Rick, architect 213
Maxwell, Sir Aymer, Knight 35
Meier, Richard, architect 205
Mendelsohn, Erich, architect 149, 167, 179

Merrilees, Andrew, architect 197
Metzstein, Isi, architect 181, 201
Meunier, John, architect 195
Middlemore, Theodosia, craftworker 121
Middlemore, Thomas, industrialist 121
Millport 12
Miralles, Enric, & Benedetta Tagliabue, architect 205, 211
Montrose 49
Morgan, John, builder and essayist 109
Morris, James, architect 185
Morris, May, craftworker, 121
Morris, William, writer, businessman, designer, craftworker, publisher 29
Mortuary Chapel *102, 103*, 107
Mott, Hay & Anderson, engineer 221
Mouchel, LG, engineer 135
Munkenbeck, Alfred, architect 205
Murphy House *218*, 219
Museum of Scotland *206*, 207
Mylne, Robert, architect 61
Mylne, Robert (II), architect 63

National Museum of Scotland 96, 97, 117
National Trust for Scotland (NTS) 53, 83
Narro, David, Associates, engineer 187
Neo-Classical architecture 55, 71, 101
Neil, Andrew, architect 163
Neil & Hurd, architect 53, 163
Netherland
  Amsterdam
    Church of the Holy Martyrs of Gorkum 171
  Den Haag 221
Netherlands (Dutch) Expressionism or Amsterdam School 125, 159, 171
Nicholl Russell Studio, architect 199
Nicholson, Ben, artist 215
Nisbet, John, smuggler 65
Nisbet, Mary, Lady Elgin, gardener 33

INDEX

Normand, Tom, art historian 159
Norway 31
    Bergen, St Mary's Church 31
    Trondheim, Nidaros Cathedral 31
Norwich
    Cathedral 89
Nyström, Alexander, architect 41

O'Donnell, Raymond, biographer 123
Orkney 12,
    Churchill Barriers 173
    Lambholm 173
    Scapa Flow 173
Outlander, television series 51

Page \ Park, architect 43, 99, 197, 213
Paisley 91
Palace of Art *168*, 169
Palumbi, Guiseppe, artisan 173
Paolozzi, Eduardo, artist 215
Patrick, Alexander, landowner 65
Paxton House *12*, *66*, 67
Paxton, Joseph, landscape architect 81
Payne, Peter, author 177
Penicuik 89
Pennisi, Giovanni, artisan 173
Pevsner, Nikolas, architectural historian 125
Picts 27
Pier Arts *214*, 215
Pilkington, Frederick, architect 89, 95, 159
Pirie, John Bridgeford, architect 105
Pitlochry 12
Pitlochry Dam *176*, 177
Playfair, James, architect 55, 73, 75
    William Henry, architect 73
Pollock Hammond Partnership, architect 149
Portugal
    Bélem, Mosteiro dos Jerónimos 43
Pre-Raphaelite Brotherhood 29
Prior, ES, architect 129, 137

ss *Queen Mary* 151
Queen's Cross Church *104*, 105
Queen Street Station 224, 225
Queensferry N&S 12, 221

Ramboll, engineer 221
RD Cameron Associates, architect 69
Reiach & Hall, architects, 187, 215
Reid Memorial Church *154*, 155
Reid, Robert, architect 67
Renaissance architecture 35, 55
Richard Murphy Architects 73, 209, 219
Richardson, Henry Hobson, architect 109
Riselaw House *132*, 133
Ritchie, Ian, architect 213
RMJM, architect 211, 213
Robert II, King of Scots 37
Rodger, Johnny, architectural historian 171
Rochead, John, architect 91
Rogers, Richard, architect 205
Romanesque architecture 29, 41
Roslin 12
Ross, Hugh, painter 145
Ross, Launcelot Hugh, architect 169
Ross, Sir William, painter 145
Ross, William HA, architect 145
Rossetti, Dante Gabriel, artist 117
Rosslyn Chapel *42*, *43*, 103
Rosyth 221
Rothesay Pavilion *166*, 167
Rothesay 12
Royal High School *72*, *73*, 85
Royal Scottish Academy 219
Roxburgh, Graham, engineer 203
Ruskin, John, artist and critic 81, 89, 109, 113, 117
Russian Constructivists 179
RW Forsyth's *138*, 139

Safdie, Moshe, architect 205
St Andrew's 12

St Andrew's House *156*, 157
St Columba, Christian missionary 41
St Conan's Kirk *106*, 107
St Cuthbert's Cooperative Society 179
St John the Evangelist RC Church *128*, *129*, 141
St Machar's Cathedral *40*, 41
St Magnus Cathedral 30, 31
St Paul's RC Church *180*, 181
St Peter-in-Chains RC Church *170*, 171
St Peter's RC Church *136*, *137*, 153, 155
St Vincent Chambers (the Hatrack) *122*, 123
St Vincent Street UP Church *84*, 85
Salisbury
    Cathedral 89
Salmon, James, architect 119, 123, 135
Sandiefield Housing *216*, 217
Sanmicheli, Michele, architect 39
Schinkel, Karl Friedrich, architect 83
Scott, Sir George Gilbert, architect 77, 83, 99, 105
Scott, Sir Walter, author 29, 91, 103
Scottish National War Memorial *152*, 153, 155
Scottish Parliament, The *210*, 211
Sedláková, Radomìra, architectural historian 51
Serlio, Sebastiano, architect 61
Sharkey, contractor 139
Shearer, James, architect 161
Shearer, Thomas Smith, architect 161
Shetland, Mousa 27
Sillitto House *184*, 185
Sim, Stewart, HM Ministry of Works, architect 179
Simon Square Housing *226*, 227
Simpson & Brown, architects 73
Sinclair, Fiona, architectural historian 105
Sinclair, William, 3rd Earl of Orkney 43
Skara Brae *16*, *17*, 19
Smith, George Gregory, literary critic

47, 89
Smith, James, architect 55
Stirling, James, architect 189
Sonck, Lars, architect 147
Spain
    Barcelona, Casa Milá 123
Spence family, farmers 45
Spence, Sir Basil, Glover & Ferguson, architect 183, 197
Stamp, Gavin, architectural historian 83
Steedman, Robert, architect 185
Steele, Matt, architect 119, 143, 147, 149
Stewart, Francis, 5th Earl of Boswell 39
Stirling 12
    High School 115
Stobo Castle 12, *68*, 69
Study, The, Culross *50*, 51
Sunderland
    St John's Roker 137
Sussex University 183

Tait, Thomas, architect 157, 169
Tankerness House *48*, 49
Tarbolton, Harold, architect 177
Taut, Bruno, architect 127
Taylor, John, architect 149
Tayport Castle 69
Telephone Exchange *178*, 177
Templeton's Carpet Factory *112*, 113
The Builder, architectural magazine 95, 137
The Building Chronicle, architectural magazine 103
Thomson, Alexander, architect 73, 83, 85, 101, 109, 201, 217
Thomson, Leslie Graham, architect 155
Three Bridges, The *220*, 221
Thurso 63
Thyssen-Bornemisza Collection 73
Tintin, strip-cartoon 37
Tobermory 63
Tomnaverie, Stone Circle 12, *22*, 23
Traquair, Phoebe Anna, artist 117
trilithon 19

270